Flirting With Madness

Louise Ellison

chipmunkapublishing
the mental health publisher

Louise Ellison

All rights reserved, no part of this publication may be reproduced by any means, electronic, mechanical photocopying, documentary, film or in any other format without prior written permission of the publisher.

>Published by
Chipmunkapublishing
PO Box 6872
Brentwood
Essex CM13 1ZT
United Kingdom

http://www.chipmunkapublishing.com

Copyright © Louise Ellison 2011

Edited by Aleks Lech

Chipmunkapublishing gratefully acknowledge the support of Arts Council England.

Author Biography

Louise Ellison is a pen name chosen to protect the identities of those she loves and the confidentiality of her profession. She is a sufferer of Obsessive Compulsive Disorder, Depression and undergone treatment for Borderline Personality Disorder. Born in 1985, in Northern England, Louise has suffered with mental illness since she was an infant and has been through the adolescent and adult mental health services.

Louise Ellison graduated from The University of Teesside with a 2:1 hons in Criminology with Law and has worked in the Criminal Justice System for over 8 years within the Prison Service and Youth Offending Service.

Heavily influenced by the new wave music and literature movement, Louise is liberal in her political views. Louise is also a keen musician who plays bass and sings a band from the north of England.

Louise Ellison

Flirting With Madness

Dedicated to my parents, who have given me so much and asked for so little.

Greg, my rock, my partner and my best friend.

Dear friends, Sarah and Frances.

Deborah and Sian for their help and patience.

May, who went to the heavens too early.

Maggie, the patient professional.

And all the sufferers of mental illness and their carers (Earth's hidden angels).

Louise Ellison

PROLOGUE

Diary entry: May 2009

It's a hard question for me to answer. How do you feel? I don't actually know for certain. I can experience a number of feelings in a short space of time - anger, happiness, euphoria, suicidal, but mostly I feel helpless and bored.

At this exact moment I feel like absolute shit. I feel angry, sad, tired and helpless. I want to punch the walls until the pain in my hands becomes so severe that I pass out. The day started normally enough and I was okay for most of it. I got out of bed around 9am (Bank Holiday sleep in) feeling a bit blue, but I am blaming that on the amount of brandy I drank last night just for the sake of it. By 9:15am I was dressed in my running gear and leaving the front door for a run. I so need to exercise. I am getting so fat. I can't believe I never realised how fat I really am. I always thought my weight was fine, but now I notice that it isn't. I keep telling myself I am being self-critical as I am 'ill,' but that does not work. I have tried to eat less the last couple of days and go hungry as long as I can. It doesn't work; I eat when I am bored and my appetite fluctuates the rest of the time. My run went okay but due to my crap fitness levels I actually walked most of the route. I came home, showered and finished reading 'Little Girl Lost,' by Lovisa Pahlson-Moller, a sufferer of Borderline Personality Disorder.

My friend Sarah picked me up from my house at about 1pm. We went to Northallerton for a coffee and a talk. I discussed with her how I am feeling; constantly masculine, angry, confused, fat, bored and desperate.

I'm fed up of being bored and feeling like this. I am bored of being bored. I am struggling to keep fighting. Even when I have good days I am upset, as I know I am not well enough for them to last.

I have not seen Maggie, my therapist, in over a week and I really need to see her, despite hating my dependency on therapy. Sarah and I discussed the fear of being 'found out.' People who I know are soon going to figure out that I am a fucking nutter or that I am really stupid and good for nothing. I feel so close to madness right now it's unbelievable. It's like I am waiting for the 'voices' to appear in my head and for the men in white coats to cart me off to some loony bin. Deep down wish I were crazy. I would not know that I am different and I could be locked up and stop hurting all my loved ones, in particular my boyfriend, Greg, and my parents.

I would love to stay in a psychiatric ward for a month or so, just enough time to have a rest, but keep my grip on reality. Imagine, no responsibility and no guilt. But that is not a possibility, as I will lose my job. Equal opportunities my arse. Break my arms and I receive flowers from the office. Yet an episode of feeling desperate and declared incompetent and I receive a P45. Never mind the fact that I understand emotional pain, the same emotional pain that drives so many to crime and anti-social behaviour. I use this experience every day as a Youth Probation Officer.

Sometimes I question whether I even want to get better, to conform to 'boring' 'conventional' society. I am guessing that may be my wee borderline trait talking. I confessed to Sarah that sometimes I 'think' I see things that are not there. For example, an injured person on the street, even though I am quite confident there is nothing there. This is very hard to hide when with friends. I think I see something and then reason with myself that it was just a mistake. Then some little internal voice puts doubt in my mind, I fight the voice and get upset because I shouldn't be thinking like that. I then go into my head and it looks to others as if I am daydreaming, when really I just want to scream. I have to concentrate to 'stay with it' and then get pissed off when others interrupt my train of thought.

Greg arrived at my home at 7pm. I was tired and in no mood to be happy. I have been drinking again over the Bank Holiday weekend and it is having depressive side affects. Greg told me he is working a week on Saturday. I got upset as he has worked the past two Bank Holidays and with our work commitments we only really get Saturdays together. I felt as though he would rather be at work than with me. I felt unimportant. I recognise that I am being unreasonable but I still had to be miserable with him and I spent the night guilt tripping him. I HATE IT WHEN I DO THIS BUT I CAN'T SEEM TO STOP, manipulation is like second nature. I really don't deserve him. He should leave me and find a real woman, one who doesn't need therapy to emotionally mature. I am so damaged, why the hell does he love me?

Louise Ellison

CHAPTER ONE

Depression and Obsessive Compulsive Disorder (OCD) were officially diagnosed to my good self when I was 18 years old. Hello, pleased to meet you. I am a hand washer, a thought ruminator, generally very pessimistic and fear the contamination of any virus or illness that could hurt a loved one or myself. I have told my close friends and my boyfriend so many times that I think I have contracted HIV that they probably deep down think I am bordering on madness.

I have always felt like I am two people, a child and an adult. Not an adult with a childish side, or even a mature child beyond her years, but actually two different people. After my third stint on anti-depressants and being told I was depressed, I got fed up. I needed to face facts; something was wrong with me that was more than depression. Why could others not see it too? Then after searching the Internet and consulting many mental health texts I found information on Borderline Personality Disorder (BPD). I fitted every symptom. I felt the phase of ignorance had, for the moment, passed. As stated by Kreisman and Straus (1989:8) the symptoms are:

- Unstable and intense interpersonal relationships
- Impulsiveness in potentially self damaging behaviours, such as substance abuse, sex, shoplifting, reckless driving, binge eating
- Severe mood swings
- Frequent and inappropriate displays of anger
- Re-occurring suicidal threats or gestures or self mutilating behaviours
- Lack of clear sense of identity
- Chronic feelings of emptiness or boredom

- Frantic efforts to avoid real or imagined abandonment.

Surely, I thought to myself, a couple of therapy sessions tailored to helping me deal with this should be sufficient and wham I will be cured, happy and content! Not that simple; Kreisman and Straus (1989:8) describe a borderline as an 'emotional haemophiliac.' I discussed BPD with a friend of mine who is a mental health nurse with the Children Adolescent Mental Health Service (CAMHS) and at the mention of the term 'borderline' he grimaced, advising that he detests working with such patients as the disorder in his opinion is 'not treatable.' Disheartened, I trawled the Internet for self help groups and therapists. I searched for anything that could get me a BPD screening without having to see my doctor and get nothing but 'happy' pills and a sick note. After visiting the web page bpdworld.com I found two therapists who worked within a thirty-mile radius of my home. Neither experts in treating BPD, but they noted knowledge of the disorder. I settled on Maggie, a self-employed counsellor with experience of treating other personality disorders, over a doctor who worked for the NHS. The doctor stated on her website that she was 'interested' in personality disorders but I am no guinea pig for anyone's interest. It's so important to find the right therapist and at 60 quid an hour cheaper, Maggie was my choice.

I hated the fact that Maggie had more power than me. I am still, good reader, learning to emotionally grow up, to live life as a fulfilled adult. However, I find myself feeling more and more like a scared and angry little girl of late, blaming and hating everyone for it. **Depression, Obsessive Compulsive Disorder (OCD) and possible Borderline Personality Disorder (BPD)**. Wow, three disorders that sum up my existence, my pain, my creativity, my self importance, my self loathing, my fears, the abuse that others have dealt with and the self abuse I continue to inflict on myself. I always knew there was something wrong, even as a small child. I believed I was destined for greatness and when it never materialised I felt delusional. I would spend time leaving reality for the comfort of my own world, but realising I was doing it. 'Daydreaming' my teachers called it, but it somehow felt so real at times and still does. Maybe I am crazy and just rather perceptive? The first time I thought I was officially crazy was when I was 20 years of age. I was walking to the bus stop from University after being in lectures all day. I noticed everything in such close detail. My senses felt heightened and I started talking to myself, wandering in my own dissociated world. I was annoyed when I had to hide such 'insanity' from passers by. I wanted to go into a fantasy world were I was happy. I then got angry with myself that I was still behaving like that at 20, like a child pretending to hold a fucking tea party. I should have been planning my career, not daydreaming and pretending I was someone else whilst walking down a public street. I toyed with the possibility that I was schizophrenic for many years; I seemed to be someone else in my head. I spent so much time trying to hide my illnesses, never telling anyone close to me my thoughts for fear of them leaving me, or even worse, colluding with my theory. The irony is that a small part of me is grateful for my illnesses. I am at least different and have an identity in this world.

******

I carefully selected feminine clothes to wear for my first meeting with Maggie but I was not in the mood to make a lot of effort in my appearance. However, I did not want to look how I felt, boyish. So nice jeans, a summer top and a three-quarter-length cardigan and one inch

heeled shoes were made to suffice. I found Maggie's flat, parked the car and proceeded to walk to her front door. I boldly rang the doorbell quickly before I changed my mind. There was no immediate answer. I panicked. She was not in. I would not get my help. I would not find out about me. Maybe I was at the wrong house? A neighbour walked by and said, 'Good Morning.'
'Morning,' I politely replied.
'Try the door bell love,' he suggested.
Yeah I hadn't thought about that, I usually just loiter until the proprietor's sixth sense kicks in and when I want to go home I click my red shoes together. (I thought such words; they never actually left my mouth.) I smiled and rang the doorbell again. Then it hit me, I looked impatient, and she was probably looking for the key. 'Oh my God,' I thought, 'I bet the neighbour knows she is a head doctor, he knows I am mad.' I wanted to run. The door opened and I was greeted by a warm smile and a 'hello.' I was shown upstairs to 'the room,' sat down and shyly waited for my session to commence. 'I must not look like a freak,' I kept telling myself. 'Act demure, keep dignity and never cry.'

We commenced the session by discussing the norms, confidentiality, expectations etc. I had heard the same introduction that Maggie gave from countless previous therapists. I was amused when she asked me if it was 'my first time in therapy?'
'No I have had many counsellors, but I am yet to complete a course of therapy,' I told her.
'Why?' she politely enquired.
'I found them useless - it never worked out.'
'Oh,' was her response.

By the end of the session it was concluded that I suffered 'Borderline Traits' and that therapy would be tailored towards this conclusion. Maggie was unable to give an official diagnosis of Borderline Personality Disorder, as she is not a psychiatrist. Since I was not prepared to go to the doctors because I was scarred of having BPD on my medical records, I made a further appointment with Maggie for the following week to start undergoing Dialectical Behavioural Therapy.

******

On 4th June 1985 at 2:05am, my mother gave the world me. I was not a pretty baby at all and I am not being modest, I really did give Quasimodo a run for his money. At four weeks premature, I had a wonky head and my right ear stuck out, looking barely attached to my face. Even the doctors and nurses who always lie and state babies are beautiful, commented on it. I had major self-image problems even then.

I don't remember much of my childhood. My first memory is being at St Joseph's Roman Catholic School afternoon nursery, where I met my first teachers, Mrs Noble and Mrs Varey. I cried and clung to my mother, pleading with her not to leave me with such strangers. She left me; I was horrified. Needless to say I eventually got over such abandonment when I was offered a toy to play with in the play area (what a fickle child I was). I struggled to mix with other children; I felt they were better than me. They always seemed one step ahead. I felt like I was playing catch up with fashion, music taste, wearing make up, my first kiss - I was always behind. I often played alone in my early school years, in my own little world. I do not recall much of this world, but it was much better than this one. I was probably Queen in mine. My only other memory of nursery is being desperate to borrow the book 'Peace At Last' from the library and being told I was not allowed. All I wanted at that moment was 'peace at last.' One could find such irony in that if one wanted to.

My memories of my infant years are not much better. I was quiet and academically average. I was by no means standing out as 'clever' or 'intelligent.' My school reports always said 'fair,' 'could do better' and 'daydreams too much.' I am upset at my lack of memories. I feel robbed. I am scared that I have blocked something out that I may one day remember. I do however recall sounds, smells and feelings. 'Heart of Glass' by Blondie was my favourite song and to this day when I hear it I feel happy; music makes me happy. I remember my parents giving me my first guitar at the age of 8. After years of pretending to play my mother's broken acoustic, they provided me with one of my own. I was ecstatic. My father wanted me to be like 'Hank Marvin' of the Shadows. We would watch videos of him in concert together when my mother was out with her friends. From a tender age I have been musically eclectic. I love everything from jazz to heavy metal. My ultimate favourite from my childhood is the late ukulele player, George Formby. 'When I am cleaning windows' was always on repeat on my beat up record player. I have many fond memories of my mother and I dancing about the living room to it.

I dreamed for hours on end of becoming a musician, writing and singing songs of my own. That dream got me through so many hard times. When things got tough, I told myself that everything would be okay because one day, music would be my saviour. When money was an issue at home and I saw my parents struggling to pay the bills I would say to myself, 'It will be okay because one day music will make me rich and my family and I will never have to worry about money again.' As I got older such fantasies did not go hand in hand with gaining GCSEs, A-levels, going to University, getting a job and basically growing old and in my head, boring. Thus now in my early twenties when I have to live in the real world, I am starting to struggle. I feel like a delusional failure.

I have no recollection of my first day of infant school, although my mother has proof the day occurred. She proudly took the photographs with me standing in the front garden with my hideous brown, yellow and white uniform that only a Catholic School could think up. (St Joseph's was obviously years ahead of Milan and Paris.) In the pictures I am standing in front of my mother's beige Ford Fiesta that she called 'Betsy'. I remember more about the car than I do my childhood. Infants / Junior School are when I started to develop a form of self-awareness. I know little about psychology, but I am confident that some of the experiences that I had at this age contributed to my psychological make up. I always felt I was different from the other children. I never had their confidence to make friends easily, but I was not too bothered at the time. My own world was fun enough. Teachers said I was distracted and withdrawn but it never caused them too much consternation, they thought I would 'grow out of it.'

CHAPTER 2

For many years I believed that I had not been sexually abused and that it was the adults in my life that were overreacting; my parents, the school, social workers and the mental health professionals. The three boys lived close to my family home. I only remember one of the boys' names, which was Robert. The other two boys were identical twins and the three of them were aged between 10 and 13. I was 6. I was in Robert's back garden with the boys and my then best friend, Shannon. Robert's father briefly came into the rear garden and discarded a cigarette, which fell onto a flowerbed before he departed, leaving the five of us alone. Robert picked up the disguarded cigarette and put it to his lips. He passed it to me and I smoked a drag of it. I had my first cigarette at 6 years old! It felt odd, I got a slight head rush and coughed really hard. There were various discussions happening between Robert, the twins and Shannon that I did not understand. I just continued 'hanging around' as they occurred. Shannon, who was two years older than me, understood. She was visibly annoyed and I could not understand why. She informed the boys that she was having no part in the proposed activities and was leaving. I did not follow, despite her requests. I did not know what had happened. I was happy to have new friends as before meeting the boys I only really had Shannon.

Robert led me to the lawn in the garden and instructed me to lie down. I did. I thought it was a game of some sort. Whilst lying on the lawn he removed my shorts and knickers. He then removed his trousers and underwear. He laid on top of me as I recall, and simulated sex with me. I cannot remember if there was any penetration as I have blocked most of it out of my memory. I started to feel scared, I felt trapped with him on top of me. I knew this game was most likely to be wrong and I panicked. Whilst lying on my back I didn't struggle; I didn't understand. I was paralysed. As this was happening the two twin boys were watching, keeping look out and laughing. For so many years I believed that it was only experimentation on Robert's part and I was not abused. I just needed to pull myself together and stop feeling like I was tainted and dirty. I told this to Maggie. She disagreed. She asked me to consider the awful things that some young people do. I do consider this as I work as a Probation Officer with youths who commit crime. I agreed with Maggie that children do commit awful and hurtful acts, but I also informed her that my training is to look at all the facts, including learned behaviour and natural curiosity. How did Robert and the twins know it was not appropriate? Then it hit me. The twins were lookouts. They had discussed it beforehand, thus there was premeditation. For years I believed it was me who was uptight and had the problem, but after dissecting the incident I now realise that they may not have understood the gravity of their actions, but they knew it was wrong.

After the incident with Robert and the twins I went home. I never socialised with those boys again and they never made the effort to socialise with me. Shannon told her mother what she had discussed with the boys and immediately her parents informed my mother and father. When I returned home, Shannon's parents were leaving the house. I felt a sudden feeling of shame. Something wrong had happened. It was confirmed by the look on my parents' faces as I entered the house. They sat me down in the living room and questioned me immediately. I was in trouble; I knew it. I had done something wrong. I should have left with Shannon, damn it. It was my fault. I was bad. I lied. I told my parents that nothing had happened and Shannon had lied because we had a disagreement. I made a promise to myself that my parents would never know and I would keep the day's events to myself. I think of the sexual abuse reports I have read whilst working in the Criminal Justice System and I consider what so many people have been through. I can only imagine how women and men who have experienced the gravity of abuse such as rape cope. My admiration is with them. However, all experiences to me are relative and make up who we become. The above experience for me, I believe, was a catalyst to my distorted thought processes and to my mental instability today. The distorted thoughts of a child can become the thoughts of an adult if not treated or addressed. I grew up feeling dirty, abused, angry, scared and feeling like I was not in control of my future. To this day I still have a huge complex about men using me!

******

'I just find it hard to be around my friends when they are all dressed up and looking really pretty.' I told Maggie. 'They look so feminine.'
'How do you feel in that situation?' Maggie asked.
'Boyish. I don't feel comfortable in my own skin. I feel on display. If I wear feminine clothes and act 'girly' I'm waiting for people to say 'who is she trying to kid?' If I receive a compliment I think it is sarcasm or that people are just accustomed to seeing me look like shit.'
'Why do you think you feel this way?' Maggie questioned.
'I just feel abnormal, I suppose. I'm not used to feeling feminine or being proud of my femininity,' I said.
'What clothes do you feel comfortable wearing?' Maggie prompted.
'Tomboyish clothes, I suppose. I long to wear feminine

clothes and act like a woman, but when I am dressed like a tomboy I feel in control. If I get judged it's because I have chosen to dress in a way that promotes it. In feminine clothes I just feel judged and vulnerable' I told Maggie.
'Vulnerable?' Maggie picked up on my lexical choice.
'Er, yes.'
'So do you think the main issue is vulnerability? Do you see femininity as vulnerability?' Maggie asked.
'I have never really thought about it. I guess so. Women tend to be the ones who get walked over or have to give things up for men' I responded.
'Do you really believe this?' Maggie questioned.
'Maybe. I don't think it should be that way, but a lot of the time it is. I feel at a disadvantage because of my sex. I would love to embrace my femininity and not see it as a weakness but I can't. I admire strong and sexy women. I would love to be that way,' I told Maggie.
'Why not be that way then? You are young, female and intelligent. What is stopping you being like the women you admire? Maggie challenged.
'It just feels so uncomfortable, exposing even' I said.
'It takes practice. You will feel more comfortable the more you do it. Think about what we have discussed today Louise and make an effort to be who you want to be, not what you think you should be and with practice the anxiety will eventually subside.' Maggie optimistically concluded the session.

******

One night, not long after my encounter with Robert and the twins, I could not sleep. I convinced my mother to allow me to stay up late with her in the living room. An appeal was on the television about a man who had sexually assaulted a young girl and as a result from the injuries sustained, she died. I asked my mother various questions about what I had seen on television. After many attempts of trying to pacify my curiosity, my mother told me that the 'man was a bad man and no girl should ever be treated in such a way.' Somewhere out of this conversation I started to think about pregnancy. I started to believe that Robert had got me pregnant and I was going to die like the girl on television. I felt trapped and that life was simply awful. I prayed everything was a dream and I would just simply wake up and everything would be okay. Sometimes I managed to convince my young impressionable mind that everything I was experiencing was a dream and that I would soon wake up in a nicer reality. Other times I would pretend to be someone else, someone famous who was not tainted or about to die through premature pregnancy. I began to detach from reality. I started to spend more time alone in my bedroom, hating myself. After a few months passed I started to realise that I was not going to die, but still believed that I was pregnant. I was worried that my parents would find out and I feared that they would no longer love me.

One summer afternoon I was riding my beautiful new Raleigh bike. (I promise you good reader it was cool at the time.) That blissful moment of riding my bike, experiencing the wind in my hair and feeling nothing but freedom was shattered when I lost control, fell against the handlebars and hit my stomach. I recalled the phantom baby in my belly. I remember thinking that the impact may have harmed the baby and one part of me was over the moon at the thought. I could be a normal girl again. The other part of me was horrified that I was capable of such horrid thoughts. I obviously deserved the pain I was in; it was a penance from God. I started to accept that I was bad and deserved everything I was going through. When I felt happy I started to experience guilt. I did not deserve to be happy.

I broke the silence at the age of 8 after two years of being miserable and hating myself. I told my mother as we sat watching a programme on the television called 'Children's Ward.' A story about a girl who had been sexually abused was aired. I could not watch. I broke down and my mother asked me if anything like that had ever happened to me. I told her. I begged her not to think badly of me and it all came flooding out. Everything I had bottled up for two years was falling and flowing like Niagara Falls. My mother remained calm, collecting the facts and comforting me, despite the look of sadness and hurt on her face. My father went ballistic. Someone had touched his little girl and he wanted retribution. To paraphrase my father, he shouted that it was no wonder Robert acted the way he did with the father he had. I did not understand this statement at the time, but later I learned that Robert's father was rumored to be a philanderer and a womaniser. I also heard rumours that he would enjoy 'threesomes' in the family home whilst Robert was in the house. My father concluded that Robert had learnt from his father and therefore it was his father's fault. My father headed towards the front door with the intention of confronting Robert's father. It took my mother to stop my father doing something stupid. To this day I remain grateful to her for that. I could not have lived with the guilt of my father being incarcerated for something he would have most likely regretted because of me.

A couple of days later I was sitting in my brother's bedroom, away from my parents, being interviewed by two social workers (one male and one female). The man sat on my brother's computer chair and the lady remained standing. I did not want to be there, I wanted to be left alone. I sat staring out of the bedroom window predicting when the next train would go past (our house was near a railway line). The social workers appeared frustrated, often having to ask me to concentrate and then seemed exasperated when I didn't say what they wanted to hear. The female social worker was wearing a very smart red jacket and I recall admiring it, I will always remember that. After interviewing me, social services were satisfied that this was a criminal matter and that the Police should conduct their own investigations. The Police interviewed Robert and I was surprised that he recalled the day in question. He told the Police that he and I were playing doctors and nurses. He lied. I may have blocked out a lot of that day, but we had certainly not been playing doctors and nurses. He was not charged. His father stated that he was close to the age of 10 at the time, either 9 or 11 years old. As I could not remember the exact date, criminal age could not be proven. Social Services closed the case.

My school was the next to find out. I sat in the Headmaster's office as he praised me for telling the truth. I just wanted to run. Was this now me, a pitied child? No longer wanting to be me, I started to daydream in order to cope. I would listen to music in my room and pretend to be the stars who sang and wrote the songs. My life would soon be okay. I would be famous, rich and worth something like all those singers who graced my record player. This detachment into daydream has stayed with me all my life to date. So much so that when my musical stardom didn't materialise I felt like a failure. It was as though I was never going to be saved and was destined to live a desperate, empty life, embarrassed by a pipe dream.

I had a lot of absences from Primary School due to my emotional difficulties at a tender age. I struggled to cope with my emotions. I would often cry for what appeared to be no reason. This embarrassed me in front of the other children. I suffered constantly with mouth ulcers and fatigue. Some ulcers were so enlarged that I struggled to eat and I was often underweight. On one occasion when I was around 9 years old I was too nervous to ask my teacher to go to the toilet and consequently wet myself in front of all my classmates. Eventually I refused to go to school. I felt too weak. As my absences became more frequent, Education Welfare Officers became involved. The officer assigned to me was Mr Wren. It was decided that I would be placed on a school reward scheme to attend more frequently. I didn't like Mr Wren. He was fat and balding and spoke to me as though I was a baby. I was emotionally suffering, not stupid. He made me a deal - if I attended school for a full six weeks he would buy me a chocolate bar. I didn't attend. I still got the chocolate bar.

Criminal Injuries Board, solicitors and psychiatric assessments followed to determine if I was eligible for compensation. This process affected me just as much as the incident itself. I can only empathise with those who are raped. What the Justice System puts them through is unacceptable. It is true that such victims are raped twice. Even as I child I felt that the solicitors and judges were trying to 'trip me up' and it was only a civil hearing. I was 12 years old when the case was heard in Durham Court and I was disgusted at having to prove my character. It made me question time and time again if I had actually suffered abuse or if I was emotionally retarded or crazy. I would cry for hours on my mother's shoulder, begging for her to help me to be 'normal.' That was always my biggest wish. I felt that I had to 'fake' being a 'normal' child and most of the time I just wanted to hide away. I tried to keep myself together at the Court but I couldn't, I cried for hours. The usher gave my mother and me a copy of the police statements that were taken when I was 8 years old. I read them and nothing would register in my mind, I felt numb. I started scratching my arms with my fingernails to distract myself from the tears welling up in my eyes. (I have always preferred physical pain to emotional pain.) It never worked. I broke down and was in too much of a state to go through with the Court hearing. In the end the Court allowed my mother to be my spokesperson as I was a minor. I was awarded £2,000. To this day I would pay 10 times that back to not have been a victim - the unified gospel truth of anyone who has suffered any type of abuse. For years after the incident I suffered bed-wetting, ulcers, depression and poor sleeping habits, which included sleepwalking. I would hide in the wardrobe when sleepwalking and beg for 'them to not let him get me.' My concerned and loving parents would tell this to all the child psychiatrists / therapists that I saw.

******

In the end my parents decided to move from the home where I had lived since I was a baby. Too many bad things had happened. I don't miss the area, but I do miss the house. I liked it. Towards the end of our residence, the area began to show signs of anti-social behaviour and poverty. I recall once playing close to someone's back garden with my brother and some other children from the Crescent where we lived. Understandably the owners of the property were annoyed with us for loitering. The man of the house came out of his home into the back garden. He screamed at us to leave. Suddenly, the older kids ran, leaving my brother and me behind. The man went into his house and returned moments later with a two-barreled shotgun. He pointed it towards us. Needless to say we ran home. Upon reaching our house we told our mother what had happened. I expected her to telephone the police. No, my mother decided to confront the man herself. After arguing with the man for sometime she reduced him to an apology and returned home rather smug. No one messes with my mother!

Another time, when I was playing in the field / beck near to our family home I came across a young man. He was about 18 years of age and sitting alone. After staring for a while I noticed that he was sniffing a white substance out of a bag. I returned home and asked my mother what it was. She didn't tell me, but she made me remain at home for the duration of the day and evening. However, the final straw for leaving the area came from our then next-door neighbour. She told a friend of my mother's that she believed mentally disabled folk should be killed at birth. This hurt my parents deeply due to my brother suffering a severe learning disability. It hurt me too. I may not have fully understood exactly what our neighbour's problem was with our family but I knew that her views were wrong. She would intimidate my brother at any given time, calling him names too ignorant to even write, or sticking two fingers up at him. She also started rumours around the estate that my father had AIDS as he was very skinny. Before we moved house I trashed her garden. I kicked over plant pots, pulled out plants by the roots, threw mud everywhere, painted her back door red and put a dent in her car bonnet. It is an action I do regret, as it was intrinsically wrong, however I don't lose sleep over it.

I have returned to the Crescent on a few occasions, usually when I am feeling low and need some answers to my mood. I often end up staring at Robert's house and remembering the events in his back garden. I still get angry that I allowed it to affect me.

Louise Ellison

CHAPTER 3

'I cut myself.' I told Maggie.
'Why?' she asked.
'I lost it; I accused Greg of flirting with someone else' I meekly said.
'Do you think he was flirting?'
'No,' I replied.
'Why do you cut, Louise?' Maggie asked.
I hated it when Maggie said my name, I felt like a child in trouble. I felt pathetic and angry all at the same time. Why do I cut? Control and relief; I don't understand how it helps, but it does. It's like I have paid my penance and can start again. 'I cut because it makes me feel better,' I said. When I cut it's always at the top of my legs on my thighs - not on my arms, as I would not want others to see that I do it. I fear I will lose Greg through this. Maggie's suggestion was to write everything down, my thoughts and feelings.
'I am concerned that I cannot treat any potential personality disorder whilst there is so much depression. It needs to come out somehow. You like words and writing, how do you feel about writing it down?' Maggie asked.
'Okay, I will give it a try' I obediently replied. I was shocked that Maggie didn't scold me for cutting myself. I felt confused.

******

I hated them all, the child psychiatrists / therapists - I thought they were patronising bastards. I hated them even more as a teenager. I believed that they got rich off my misery and I dreaded going to see them. If an appointment loomed I could not concentrate or relax for many days prior. I would panic that they would think I was crazy. They would separate me from my family by locking me up. I couldn't live without my parents. As I got older I started to realise that my parents were not immortal. I worried especially about my mother's mortality. She was my primary care giver, the one I relied upon to look after me, and the one I have always admired. If she went out I would stand by the window watching and waiting for her to return. If she were five minutes late I would cry uncontrollably and panic that she had died and that I had been abandoned. Who would look after me? Who would protect me? Did she not know how I would suffer if she left? Then I would hear her come home and I would quickly rush to bed and pretend to be asleep. At about the age of 11 or 12 I told myself that if my mother died before me I would kill myself. I told this to my parents and to the mental health professionals - they were appalled.

A female child psychologist I visited as a teenager would ask me to draw pictures of the boy who abused me and of my feelings. I refused to partake in such artistic expression. I told her I felt it was babyish but I was happy to write down my feelings, as I like words. She agreed to this and asked me to write my thoughts and feelings on her computer so she could keep a copy. I then spent nearly a whole session showing her how to use basic programmes on her computer. Other times she would like to play board games with me. This gave her the opportunity to talk to me. I felt it was tactically underhand. I just wished that they would get to know me in my own time and allow me to build up trust.

I was referred to a psychiatric hospital as an outpatient to see a specialist at the age of 13. I remember sitting in the waiting room with my mother, again just wishing the session over. My name was called and I had to go and see a male psychiatrist on my own. I remember him being very geeky looking and appeared more suited to IT than working with 'emotional' young people. He asked me the same questions that most other mental health practitioners had asked, but he was more concerned over my suicidal thoughts. I didn't have tendencies, just thoughts, I have always deep down just wanted to live and be happy. His recommendation was extensive therapy. I refused to engage. For many years I still maintained that I would kill myself if anything happened to my mother.

******

'Would you like a glass of water?' Maggie asked this every session. It annoyed the hell out of me as every time I declined. I then stared about the room and rubbed my hands together for something to do.
'So how do you see yourself?' she asked
'Pardon, in what way?' I questioned.
'When you look in the mirror, what do you see and feel?'
'Well I'm intelligent, slightly arrogant and a bit emotionally retarded. I don't like what I see; I wish I were someone else' I replied.
'Wow.' Maggie said that a lot.
I continued to stare around the room feeling uncomfortable, wanting to leave and stay at the same time.
'What do you think about borderline personality disorder?' she calmly asked.
'Well, it sucks quiet frankly; at least I know what might be wrong, the more I learn, the more I become text book. At least I have an identity for the first time in my life,' I said.
Maggie nodded and I started to worry that she thought I didn't have BPD and that I was a fake who just wanted attention. I began to wonder if she had ever worked with a borderline before. I didn't want her to have worked with other borderlines. I didn't want to be

second.

'So how do you see yourself at work?' Maggie interrupted my thoughts.

'At work I am fine, I actually feel human there. I am somebody and overall I enjoy my job. I get good feedback, have progressed very quickly for my age and get paid well,' I said.

'You must be very proud of that,' Maggie replied.

'Yeah until they find out that I am a fraud and that I have just managed to fool them this long. I hate it, I always feel lucky rather than competent. It's like I can't relax, I am waiting to be found out,' I moaned.

'Wow - that is borderline, isn't it?' Maggie concluded.

******

I was an uncomfortable teenager, but I certainly enjoyed these years much more than my younger ones. I still had many emotional hang-ups but I had learnt to hide them well from most of my friends; only a few close friends and my family who took me to therapy knew. By the age of 13 I had a friendship group who cared about me and I them. I went to an excellent secondary school with teachers who liked me and developed my academic ability. I entered St Michael's Roman Catholic School at the age of 11 years old with only basic skills in reading and writing. I had missed so much primary school due to emotional problems that my education had suffered. I was academically behind all the other kids as I could barely write legibly and still had to use a pencil. I was not 'ready' to be trusted with a pen. Not that it mattered to me at the time. I was going to be a rock star. I was playing the guitar (badly) and the only subject I took to very quickly at St Michael's was music. My first music teacher was Miss Parker, a complete nutter. Eccentric didn't do her justice and I adored her. She had wacky hair, weird glasses and always nodded her head dramatically to the music when teaching music appreciation.

The first parents' evening at St Michael's indicated that I was behind the other students. My Science teacher, Mr Doherty told my parents that all the revision in the world would not help me. (Ironically by the age of 16 I was one of only ten students in the school year to study higher, triple award science at GCSE and I went onto study science at A-Level.) However I am glad Mr Doherty said what he did. I was so determined to prove him wrong. I didn't like people thinking I was 'thick' or 'foolish', even if I was academically behind. I recall being around a friend's house one evening and she and her father were reading a fact book. I was jealous that she understood so much more than me. I made a decision that night. I was bored with being academically challenged. I was going to make an effort to study and re-invent myself into a smarter person. In my second year of secondary school I started to listen more and pay attention. Teachers noticed and devoted more time to me. It was not long before I was academically performing at the top end of my class. I was called 'swot' by some, but I didn't care, I actually had a brain and was starting to realise that knowledge and education were very important tools.

By my final two years at school I had managed to progress to all the 'top sets' of my classes, even French, which I hated. I was entered for all higher papers for my examinations, with the exception of Textiles, which was way too girly for me to apply myself to or even show an interest in. I enjoyed studying extra Science after school, along with staying back after hours to indulge in additional music classes and to coach the girls' football team with two dear friends, Sarah and May. However, I never felt satisfied. I resented the typical 'female' role of society, which despite all the 'equal rights' bullshit still exists. I felt like George Eliot at school, feeling guilty about my academic ambition. I was a walking parody. I didn't want to fit into to society's norms, but yet I craved acceptance.

Apart from the 'D' grade in Textiles, I gained all A*-B passes at GCSE. I was proud of my achievements but it never felt like enough. I always felt like I was lucky to have achieved the grades, I didn't deserve them. I always felt like I was 'faking it.' I felt that I only got good grades because I revised well or because the right questions came up on the exam paper. The media attention about exams being too easy only fuelled my thoughts about my 'fake intelligence.' Even today I feel put on the spot when I am told I am good at something because I feel the need to live up to that perception, and now that it has been noted I will be observed and found out as a fake. Perception has always been a difficult thing for me. At College we discussed David Hume's philosophical theory that each human being is only a bundle of perceptions. I often think about this. Is my reality the same as others? Or is reality relative to perception and am I only intelligent if other people perceive me to be? This again goes back to my worry that I am crazy, that I think and perceive things differently to others. Do others get bogged down with such thinking? Or am I thinking myself crazy? "I think therefore I am." Rene Descartes may have been as 'mad' as me!

I was never outrageous at school or particularly openly rebellious; I was a closet rebel, yet I longed to be a rebel in the open. By my teens I had discovered the New York Punk Scene of the 1970s. I aspired to be like Debbie Harry of Blondie, a tough chick, musical and intelligent. Whilst all my pals were swooning over boy

bands I just wanted to learn more about Punk and New Wave music. I read for hours about the New York club CBGBs, Blondie, The Talking Heads, The Ramones, Bowie, Iggy, Souixsie and the Banshees - the list goes on. I loved their attitude - tough and not taking shit from anyone. I wanted to be like them, protect myself from the hard world. I started to experiment with my dress sense and black became the norm. Baggy clothes hid my feminine yet skinny frame and I looked and felt a little boyish. Part of me loved my style, yet another part of me loathed it, but like I told Maggie, my life is sometimes like a car crash. I see it coming but can't get out of the way fast enough. One day I remember sobbing on my bed screaming at my mother, 'Do you think I want to be like this, this miserable Goth?'
'Well, don't' she replied.
I was so upset. I felt no one understood, I mean, how could anyone? I was so fucked up. I may have felt boyish, but at least I never felt vulnerable, despite the unwanted attention that came with the choice of dress. When I dressed wacky I never wanted others to stare, in fact it slightly annoyed me. I hated those who judged me, but at the same time I envied their position to judge.

As a teenager I always wanted to be part of a band. I was desperate to express myself through music. From the age of 11 until the age of 16 I was involved in the school choir, guitar ensemble and I studied music at GCSE level, which bound me to be involved in all school concerts and orchestral duties. I recall being approximately 15 years of age when I was watching one of the school bands playing at the Christmas concert. They were fantastic; beautiful melodies, powerful drum beats, rock riffs and vocals full of attitude. Half way through the performance (that I was actually enjoying), I had an overwhelming urge to cry. That band had what I desperately wanted: an avenue to express themselves, a band and identity to belong to. I looked down at the guitar I was holding ready to play 'Santa Claus Is Coming To Town' with the ensemble. All I wanted to do was smash the guitar on the floor. I was never going to be in a band, I was never going to be accepted. I just about got through the festive song with the other guitarists.

Eventually I did form a band during my final year in Secondary School named 'Restless Rubbish,' and in all fairness the name was accurate. The band did not last, but we did have a good song called, 'Why?' My friend, Amy described the sound of the song as 'The Beatles' on amphetamines. Personally I thought it sounded great! My friend Sarah and I went to a music festival one wet weekend to celebrate the success of Restless Rubbish. It was here Sarah and I first saw the band, 'Proud Mary' and quickly became obsessed. Somewhere out of this obsession Sarah and I started our own band. We had one devout fan who was an IT assistant who would loiter outside the practice room as we rehearsed our only song, 'I Have Another.' I was convinced our band would become the biggest band in the world. Sarah only wanted to be in a band to attract a fellow musician who she thought was 'lush.' Unsurprisingly our band broke up, although approximately one year ago we had a brief reunion and penned our second hit, 'He's A Nymph.'

******

It was about the age of 15 that I got involved with religion in an unproductive way. I spent a significant amount of time praying that God would save me from myself. I was waiting for Him to validate my identity. I needed Him to make me pure again so no one would care that I had been sexually abused or that I was crazy. Thus I needed to be 'good' and 'pure' at all times. I put so much pressure on myself to be virtuous, to be 'cured' that it sent me over the edge.

I started to attend School Chapel every lunch time and I would venture to St Mary's Church every Sunday. However, I could not bring myself to receive Holy Communion as my thoughts were not pure enough when sitting in the pews in Church. To take the Eucharist would be blasphemy. The more I tried to keep my thoughts pure the more sexual and perverse they became. I was so ashamed of myself. How could anyone who thought about masturbation and sex in Church be saved and pure? Eventually I came to the conclusion that I was too sinful for Church so I stopped attending. I left the Church convinced that if I kept attending and offending God I would definitely burn in hell.

It was around this time that I started seeing my first boyfriend. I never took the relationship seriously as I viewed girls who got upset by boys as pathetic. Surely now was time to have fun and love to me at 15 / 16 was only an illusion. His name was James. We had been close friends for a few years and I actually trusted him more than other boys in my school year as he accepted me from day one. He never questioned the way I dressed, my tomboyish ways and seemed to understand me rather well. I was rubbish with most boys, I could never talk to them in 'that' way, and I was always the 'best friend'. Most of my peers growing up were boys and I always wanted to be a boy when I was a kid. Boys had fun; action men, climbing trees, football, play fights, etc. I hated been governed by fucked up emotions and the boys I knew never appeared to be emotionally suffering. Thus I believe it fair to conclude that I blamed my fragile emotional state on my sex. I remember once being in a pastoral class at school and a male friend of mine said 'I hate the girls in this class, a proper bunch of sluts.' I looked at him dumbfounded and he replied, 'Oh I didn't mean you, I mean you are one of us, one of the boys.' I was hurt. Despite hating my femininity I wanted to be desirable and seen as one of the girls, to be viewed as sexy. I loved the fact that James loved me. I never doubted it as he was like a puppy dog. He always wanted to spend time with me and would drop anything at a moment's notice for me. I actually believed that this is how love should be. If a man loved me this is how he should act to stay on his pedestal.

When James and I got together my parents were shocked, but I think they were a little relieved as I am of the opinion that they felt it was a sign I was moving on with my life. However I hadn't got over past issues; I had developed some different form of mental thinking to cope. I always knew I had a different perspective on things and my first relationship highlighted this. My brain went into overdrive. I had a strong urge to control and manipulate the relationship and not have him control me. I guess I had, and still have if I am honest, control issues. I hate to admit that upon reflection I acknowledge that I would emotionally manipulate James, flip into anger fits for nothing and would over react to everything. If he followed me around like a puppy dog and I was in a bad mood I would shout and get angry at him. If he didn't follow me around like a puppy dog I accused him of not caring. I remember once James was play fighting with me and I accidentally kicked him in his groin. He wanted me to apologise as he was in rather a lot of pain. I got angry and stated that he should not have started it. He left my home upset and I followed him. I eventually caught up with him and shouted that if he didn't like my personality or accept responsibility for starting the disagreement then he should get lost. As predicted he apologised and begged me not to leave him. That made me satisfied.

As a teenager one of my favourite places to 'hang out' was under the fly over bridge close to my home. I would love to go 'investigating' under this bridge with my friends. I would try and figure out about other people from what rubbish was discarded, or what conspiracy theories the rubbish may point to. The only evidence was that of homeless folk and teenagers drinking and smoking cannabis with home made bongs. I liked the privacy from the outside world there. During the afternoon before the drinkers and drug users arrived the place was quiet. I loved to listen to the traffic driving overhead, it was very therapeutic. On one occasion I took James to my little sanctuary. We were kissing and things got a little frisky. I recall him taking my top off and some lads walked by and caught us. I was wearing a bright red bra that was not entirely discreet. I grabbed my top and James and I ran. He was so embarrassed. I found it hilarious, I felt so excited and alive.

At the age of 16 I was forwarded for a summer University programme as the school saw me as 'intelligent' and 'academic.' I agreed to go. I was proud to be considered. When I arrived on the programme on the first day I immediately felt intimidated by all the clever teenagers there. I felt out of place. The only person I gelled with was a lad called John. He seemed as uncomfortable with himself as I did. Despite having a boyfriend in James I was attracted to John; he was clever, alternative and witty (even if his website was called '101 Ways To Slash Your Wrists'). By the end of the first day at the University John asked me out on a date. I wanted to go but I declined as I was with James. When I got home I had a fight with James so told him about John. I told James that it was all his fault as he did not treat me right. James cried and told me he was sorry for 'neglecting' me. At the time I honestly believed everything was James' fault and I was the victim. At 16 I thought I was just a teenager. I now realise it was my manipulation that ended our relationship.

There was a lot of pressure to have sex at 16. I felt the pressure, only I was petrified of falling pregnant. I fooled around and stuck to heavy petting, which was enough for me. The first time I ever received oral sex from James I flipped, screamed and cried. I then asked him to leave my room and made him feel like shit. I felt dirty and cheap and started to worry that I had somehow become pregnant. I was such a neurotic girlfriend. Thus James and I had a turbulent relationship and we would break up and get back together all the time. When we split for good I sunk into a deep depression. Not because I had lost the love of my life, but because I hated myself for the way I treated him. I began to feel that I was no different from Robert who had sexually abused me. You hear all the time that the abused go on to be abusers. If I fell into that category I wanted to be dead. I worried that I may have touched James in the course of our relationship in a way that had made him uncomfortable. Despite us splitting I would phone him all the time to apologise for anything I may have done sexually that made him uncomfortable. He would spend hours reassuring me that he had consented to all sexual acts that we had participated in. He would beg me to stop hurting myself emotionally. He would tell me he still loved me and that he missed me. I liked the attention and if he loved me then I couldn't be a bad person. Eventually he got fed up with reassuring me and informed me he could not cope with my emotional needs and asked me to leave him alone to move on. Our mutual friends started to ignore me and by the time

Flirting With Madness

James and I started college I was lonely and confused. I started to believe that James had decided that I had been sexually inappropriate and I was some sex offender or something. I would get angry with myself for being irrational and 'crazy.' I was knackered most of the time and during periods of exhaustion I would again worry that I had fallen pregnant before James and I had parted ways. I knew deep down my reality was distorted and I constantly fought myself in my head to believe reason. I would at times wish to go crazy and 'let go.' I started to become narcissistic and believed that I was special enough to get pregnant in a different way to others, that I was chosen, or that God was punishing me for being a 'bad' person. All the panic and worrying affected my menstrual cycle. This in my mind was confirmation that I was indeed pregnant. I was so confused and trapped. I couldn't even contemplate suicide because I don't morally believe in harming an unborn child. I instead decided to self loathe for months. Eventually my periods returned. I wasn't pregnant after all. Surprised?

******

Throughout college my dress sense fluctuated dramatically from week to week. I dressed very punky, gothic, indie, trendy and even masculine. I was struggling to feel acceptance. One day I turned up to college wearing a white shirt, black tie, black trousers, black boots, a suede jacket and a brown cowboy hat. I got a lot of looks and earned various nicknames such as 'Jon Bon' (after Jon Bon Jovi) and 'Dick Tracy.' I became known for my 'statements of dress.' I would spend weekends trawling charity shops for my next wacky outfit. It was around this time that I discovered the local punk club. Every Friday night from the age of 16 - 19 I went to a club called the Georgian Theatre. It was an alternative / underground club that on Friday nights had a themed 'trashed' night that would cater to the underground masses. Punk, rock, emo and metal music would be played to a black hole in the wall. It was here approx 100 - 200 misfits would meet and dance (well mosh and pogo) the night away. When I was under 18 years of age (and physically looking about 13) I would get a friend to buy me a hip flask of vodka on the way home from college and I would get intoxicated before going out on the town. By the time I reached the club I would be very drunk, full of 'confidence' and dance.

One time I consumed too much alcohol before I went out. I was waiting for my mate to come to my house before we ventured off to the club together. I was watching the film, 'The Craft' whilst getting ready. I was unable to watch the TV screen due to my blurred vision. When my mate arrived I excused myself to the bathroom. I sat on the bathroom floor and laid my head on the toilet seat. I heard banging on the door and my mate was begging me to come out, which I did. It turned out I had been in the bathroom over an hour and had passed out. I was scared. This had never happened to me before. I had suffered an alcohol induced blackout. I staggered into the living room where my father was and I burst into tears and fell over the coffee table. I sobbed for about another hour, feeling helpless. Then I suddenly got up and stated that I felt fine. My friend and I went to the club and I felt as happy as Larry (whoever he is). By the end of the night I was feeling euphoric and had put the blackout behind me.

I loved the Friday nights at the Georgian Theatre, not because the place was great, but the scene at that time was good. Every weekend I seemed to have a different bloke in my life. It was a joke with my peers that I was a 'serial dater.' I loved 'pulling' and proving I was likable enough to attract attention, but I would get bored easily. I went through a series of 'brief' affairs but always craved more attention. The guys I dated at that time were not particularly the 'crème de la crème.' Most were drops outs, potheads or wasters, but I needed their attention to feel good about myself, for my sense of worth. Despite jumping from loser to loser I still loved the scene. I was a young person obsessed with the New York punk scene and I felt like I had my own CBGBs on the doorstep.

I also loved being drunk. I felt confident and secure in my skin. It is a shame it never lasted and always resulted in a hangover. When my mother would go out and my father went to bed I would go into the living room and open the liquor cabinet and find the strongest spirit that my mother wouldn't notice missing. Later I would top the bottle back up with water. I would get drunk and sit down alone in the living room. Usually I ended up crying, sometimes without even knowing why, I just felt helpless. Then I would go to bed and wait for my mother to return home, crying if she were late.

CHAPTER 4

Diary Entry: 09.05.09 - 4:25pm

I feel like killing myself, ending it all - all this sadness, hurt and anger. What is the point? Teleologically it would provide more happiness. My loved ones, friends and colleagues would no longer have to put up with my mood swings, manipulative behaviour and damn right childish emotions. Not that I will kill myself today or any time soon (if ever). It takes courage and guts. I will never have that. I remain a coward and a slave to my damned childish emotions.

It's 5 years this week since May killed herself. I wonder to this day how she must have felt to do such a thing. What did she believe in her final moments of life? Maybe one day in the next life she will tell me. I feel so depressed today and so fat. I'm trying not to eat. I wish I had the guts to starve myself. I need to lose some weight. I skipped breakfast and so far have only had a sandwich to eat - it's 4:30pm so I suppose that is not too bad. My energy is low (not helped by not eating I know) and I have a strong urge to cut myself. I can't, no time alone. Even as I write Greg is lying down next to me. I HATE MYSELF, I JUST WANT TO HURT. I wish I could just cross the border, go crazy and get locked up. I constantly fantasise about being hospitalised, about being looked after. Fully looked after, even if were just for a month or so. No responsibility, no guilt, no anger - nothing.

******

I was getting really annoyed with my Criminology reading when the telephone rang. It was Donna, a friend whom I had known since school, but had not

spoken to in a while. I therefore knew it must be bad news. 'I'm sorry to be the one that has to tell you this, but May is dead.' Donna said.
'How?' I quickly asked.
'Oh Louise, she killed herself.' Donna cried.
I remained quiet for what felt like eternity. 'How did she do it? Did she at least leave a note?' I asked.
'I don't know how, Lou. No, she left no note,' she said.

I was so angry at May. No explanation, nothing. Then I felt guilty; I should have known something was wrong. God, she must have been in so much pain. I was puzzled by the lack of a suicide note. May always liked attention. Maybe it was a cry for help gone wrong? I could only ponder. I first met May in secondary school through the girls' football team along with my other peer Sarah. At weekends between the ages of 15-17, May, Sarah and I would meet up and venture into the local town dressed up as punk rockers or Goths. We would just 'hang out' in the town's streets. May always went a little further than Sarah and me, expressing a more 'shocking' dress sense. I recall on one occasion May purchasing a pair of red contact lenses and wearing them all day in public. We got some looks that day. May was always the one who would challenge people's dirty looks and many times Sarah had to pull May away from a potential altercation. Sarah and I would not opt to fight, we would just sit in the House of Fraser coffee shop dressed like punks, talk really loud and pretend that we were in town to score drugs or that we had just got out of jail for being violent. We would laugh ourselves silly when people would look at us horrified, quickly drink their tea and leave the shop. Many people judged us and we gave them what they expected.

When Sarah and I went to college, May joined the Army. At first she seemed happy, writing to Sarah and I about her regime and her ambitions for the future. Then after a short time she would telephone and say that she wanted to come home. She told me once that she had been trying to get medically discharged as she had a bad shoulder and didn't feel fit for duty. She was never discharged. I was 18 years old, nearly 19 when May took her life. I read speculation in the local and national press that there was an investigation into the cause of death. Some believed May was murdered and it was made to look like suicide. It transpired that May was being bullied in the Army. She never told me.

On the day of May's funeral I had a Criminal Law exam at University. Her funeral was in the morning and the exam in the afternoon. I never told anyone at University, I just wanted to get by. It was about this time that I was medicated with anti-depressants for the first time, with a pill known as Sertraline, and it made me very drowsy. May's funeral was awful. I couldn't believe she was dead. The last time we spoke we had an argument after she told me that she had 'punched someone.' I told her I didn't believe in violence and the argument went from there. She never telephoned me again and 6 weeks later she was dead. Allegedly she hanged herself with a tie from her door handle in the Army barracks. If only I had seen the signs. If only I saw that her anger was a cry for help. Part of me will always have to live with that. I couldn't cope in the funeral service and I broke down in the Church, practically falling to my knees. Fortunately my mother was there to support me throughout.

After the funeral, I returned home, got dressed and then went to University to sit my Criminal Law exam. I felt numb. I just sat in the exam hall feeling empty and tired. I felt the anti-depressants kicking in. I felt sick. Half way through the exam paper the tiredness got too much. I put my head on the desk and fell asleep for about twenty minutes. My peers assumed I was pulling some stunt. I wasn't. I had physically and emotionally shut down. Miraculously I still passed the exam. The inquest into May's death was concluded as suicide. The last I heard her mother was still campaigning for the case to be re-opened.

******

Sarah and I would go out most weekends when we were 15-16 years of age to get drunk and party. At the time I thought we were super cool and first class rebels. To some extent I guess we were. If we went out on a Friday or Saturday night together we would go to the Georgian punk night or to a lad's house party that we knew from school. The boys who went to the party looked slightly older than their ages and could get served alcohol in the local off licence. Sarah and I were usually the only girls at the party and therefore we would get the male attention whilst getting drunk. I loved it. On one occasion, Sarah drank so much that she grabbed hold of the house's drainpipe whilst leaving through the front door and pulled down the guttering and nearby gazebo. She then fell into the parked car on the driveway, nearly breaking its rear windscreen. I laughed so hard I thought my sides would split. Sarah just lay there on the driveway pissed.

It was at one of these parties that I got involved with a lad called Joseph. I had known him for a while as we went to the same school and he was the ex boyfriend of my friend, Amy. (I should never have gone there, I know.) He invited me to his home one day whilst his parents were out and I accepted the invitation. When I arrived at his home we went upstairs to his bedroom and started to fool around, nothing too heavy, just kissing and fondling. Suddenly Joseph got up off the bed and stated that he was going downstairs for a drink. When he left the room I proceeded to have a nosey around. I found plenty of pornography and approximately 30 empty cans of larger under the bed and on the floor. Joseph startled me when he came back into the room. 'My mother thinks I am an alcoholic,' was all he said. His demeanour changed and he went quiet, then out of nowhere he took a screwdriver out of his pocket. He used the tool to take off the door handle on the bedroom door. Then he locked the door using the screwdriver. He said it was to prevent us being 'disturbed.' I started to panic. Shit, what situation had I put myself in? I mentally prepared myself to fight when he put a video on the VHS player. It was 'Queen's Greatest Hits.' He then ignored me for the rest of the video and looked longingly at Freddy Mercury on the TV screen. Afterwards he walked me home. I broke up with him immediately.

Other times Sarah and I would go to this man's house. The man was in his late 30s. He would let us watch television and drink booze whilst he smoked cannabis and watched pornography. At the time I thought it was brilliant. I was living life to the full, taking risks and rebelling. I thought the bloke was harmless as he only made sexual comments and never tried anything physical. As I write now as an adult I cannot believe the naivety that I had. Sarah and I were lucky as our rebellion placed us in a potentially vulnerable position.

The latter was not an isolated incident. I did a lot of stupid things towards the end of my teens just to feel rebellious and alive. Once, whilst absolutely hammered on spirits, I got into a car with a man I didn't know after speaking to him for only an hour in a bar. To illustrate further my sense and sensibility when he dropped me off at the end of my road I asked him to get out of the car with me. I proceeded to push him up against the car and kiss him. I then pushed him up against a fence, which broke. There I was, 17 years of age, pissed out of my brains in a car with a bloke a good few years older than me whom I did not know. I could have been raped, murdered or both, yet I didn't care. Working in the job I do, I see a lot of young girls who act in a similar way. I spend so much time trying to convince them to look after their own safety and not to act the way I did. I just hope that something I say does actually sink into their thoughts.

I just always wanted to push boundaries in my teens, like most teenagers, but I never felt I pushed them enough. My friends called me 'wild,' but I was a closet rebel with those in authority and I needed to go further. I always longed to be wilder and wilder, I hated being boring. One Friday night when I was 18 years old I was leaving a punk club with some friends to catch the last bus home. We walked to the park, which was opposite the club and directly in front and in full view of the local police station. It was here we decided to sit down and smoke cannabis. Part of me was thrilled; it was a finger up to authority. The other part of me was a little concerned about the path I was walking.

I also liked pushing the boundaries of personal danger and still do to some extent. It makes me feel alive. I love walking alone in the dark and being in the more dangerous parts of town; I feel the adrenaline pumping. After my punk rock nights on Fridays I would on many occasions walk home alone through rough streets known for anti-social behaviour. My friends would beg me to get a taxi or catch the last bus. I would lie and pretend to do so, but I rarely did. The walk home involved walking down alleyways with no street lighting, rough estates and fields, whilst heavily intoxicated on cheap supermarket brand alcohol. I felt so alive for a brief moment. I felt danger and my instincts would kick in, telling me I wanted to live. I had the urge to survive. Once when walking home on one of these dark nights I was approached by a young man who was about 18 years old. He asked me for money. He could barely stand up straight, his eyes were blood shot and he was holding his left arm. He told me that he needed 'gear.' I politely told him that I did not have any money for him. He stated that a cigarette would suffice. I again told him I was unable to help. He started coming closer towards me and looked angry. He shouted that I was a 'no good whore.' I started to run but I was wearing heels and could not move very fast. Fortunately the man was so intoxicated that he fell against a wall and I was able to get out of sight.

Another time, more recently, I went to see Blondie and The Stranglers live in Liverpool. I told myself that I needed to be drunk to enjoy the gig, as it was rock and roll. I was so happy that I was staying in the same hotel as The Stranglers and Blondie. Whilst having a drink in the hotel bar The Stranglers came and also had a bevy. I felt like rock and roll royalty. By the end of the evening I was so drunk I could barely stand. Greg was not too happy as I recall. Whilst waiting for a taxi I nearly fell into Albert Docks. After Greg caught me in time he decided that a taxi would take too long and he carried me back to the hotel. He was rather upset and kept asking me to think about what would have happened if he had not caught me in time. It did not occur to me at the time I could have drowned. I did however pay for the alcohol consumption the next day when I had to travel three hours on National Express with a hangover. Although I was not as bad as last time I went to see 'Blondie' with 'Little Fish' in Newcastle. I was so drunk I could not stand up straight and I kept grabbing at Greg's jeans to stabilise myself. He was so pissed off at me as on one occasion I pulled his jeans down to reveal his boxer shorts.

******

Believe it or not good reader I am actually high functioning in the work place. Unless I told you I was a neurotic mess you would not know to meet me. You will see me sat in the boardroom, at multi-agency meetings or giving evidence in Court as a Youth Justice Professional. I have become a marvelous liar regarding my emotions but I am told I am good at my job. I work as a Probation Officer for youths between the ages of 10 and 18. Prior to that I was an Executive Officer in Her Majesty's Prison Service, serving as a line manager to the prison's Resettlement Department. I am very passionate about my work, and I am proud that I provide help and support to those who society often forget about and judge. Everyone makes mistakes and we all deserve chance after chance to become better people. The best thing about my job is that I get to help young people who are sometimes just in need of help. Youths get a lot of negative press attention in modern society and the term 'Broken Britain' is used almost daily within the media. Don't get me wrong; some of the young people I work with are very dangerous and need incarceration, but most just need support. I guess crime acts like a support network for them.

One of the first girls I ever worked with was 13 years of age and she was called Lexy. She had committed fraud in that she had used her mother's credit card on the Internet without permission. Upon meeting with Lexy it was clear that she was intelligent and articulate but unhappy. She seemed so lost in this big bad world.

She was bullied at school and constantly worried about her autistic brother. After a few meetings with her I took her to a place where counselling was offered to young people with caring responsibilities. She accepted the referral and was placed on the waiting list. She thanked me for believing that she was more than a thief. After that I picked her up from her home once a week and took her to the beach for an ice cream and a chat. Very quickly I noticed her confidence increase, and when her counselling came through I discharged Lexy from the Youth Offending Service. After a couple of weeks I received a telephone call from Lexy's mother telling me that Lexy was like a different girl and she believed I was her 'guardian angel.' Probation Officers do make a difference. The few we do help along the way make it worthwhile. Those with mental health difficulties also need guardian angels. We are all struggling in this world.

CHAPTER FIVE

Dissociation is the ninth criteria for BPD, which has been accepted as a further symptom of the disorder to that stated earlier in this literature, as listed in the Diagnostic and Statistical Manual of Mental Health Disorders of the American Psychiatric Association diagnosis of BPD. A Dissociative Episode is described in Friedel's book 'Borderline Personality Disorder Demystified' as "periods of time when thinking, behaviour and memory occur outside a person's normal awareness." (2004:214)

I knew I had elements of the above when I first read about it; this is mostly why I felt I was crazy. I believed everyone suffered dissociation but hid it better than me or never let it bother them. I sometimes think dreams are real, or I take a long time to decide if a memory is in fact that or a fabrication of my mind, or sometimes I think that a fabrication of my mind is a real memory. When I am really ill I think that I am singled out and that natural law may not apply to me. As a teenager I believed I was pregnant despite being a virgin. I was certain God was punishing me or had some special plan for me as I was different to 'normal' folk. Sometimes I will drive home, enter my home and completely forget how I got there. Other times I will look at the clock and then after looking again after what I think to be ten minutes and hours have passed. I cannot account for the time passed, it's as if I have forgotten. I guess we all have some elements of the above, however throughout my research I have gained knowledge of my condition and realise that I dissociate almost daily. My experience involves detaching and, well, talking to myself. I don't hear voices, I don't think I am someone else and I don't think I am talking to anyone. I know I am talking to myself but on occasions I get so caught up in my fantasies that it takes me a while to 'come back down to earth.' When alone I pretend to be someone else or pretend I am a more confident Louise talking to others. It helps me cope. It's like a little girl who plays with her dolls and pretends to be all the characters. For example, I will get angry with someone and say nothing, as I do not feel comfortable to do so at the time of the disagreement. When alone I will pretend I am talking to them and giving them a piece of my mind. I talk out loud and get lost in 'daydream / fantasy.' I start believing I have actually had the 'made up' conversation. If I am really struggling with my mental health I will pretend I am someone else and talk out loud as that person and live in their 'world.' It can be people I know or even famous people. Sometimes I can do this for hours and not realise I am doing it for this length of time. It's rather embarrassing when people catch me and I have to pretend that I am singing or mumbling about some report I have to write for work. 'First sign of madness you know, talking to yourself.' If only they knew.

Diary Entry: 10.05.09

Today was better than yesterday mood wise. No suicide thoughts at least. I did however self-harm again. I took scissors to the top of my left arm. They were blunt and I didn't have the heart to push down hard. I was not feeling that emotionally stressed but I actually wanted to cut myself. It's like a weird indulgence.

I am now starting to sober up. I have been drinking Brandy all afternoon, so am feeling a little sick now. I played on the guitar today, which was great but also awful. It makes me realise how much I want a creative career rather than a boring, normal 9-5 existence.

Nothing else to report. Feelings of boredom, intoxication and discontent, but at least I feel much better than yesterday. What a fucking wasted weekend. I feel really groggy at the moment. I guess the Brandy is kicking in. I'm much better than I was, I keep telling myself.

Do I want to get better? Funny question. Do I want to remain mentally ill? There is a part of me that does, if I am honest. To remain interesting and against the norm. However I am beginning to realise that the real world may not be much but I long to be a part of it.

Diary Entry: 14.05.09

Maggie cancelled today. I was gutted and even more gutted that I was gutted. I felt that I had hit rock bottom, and was dependent on therapy. I had lots to talk about. I feel so helpless. I attempted to cut again last night, but my scissors are really blunt and as I hate pressing down I only managed superficial cuts. I found myself planning to buy sharp scissors for the future. I HATE PLANNING LIKE THIS. For years I have put up with difficult situations and I never resorted to cutting like this. Why has it got so bad?

Last night I drank myself into a stupor and ate seven bags of crisps in a row. I felt so ill and upset as I need to lose weight - I am so fat. It is five years tomorrow since May died. I have been thinking about May a lot lately. I miss her, pity her and admire her at the same time. I actually understand the guts that she must have had to end her life, yet I hate her more for leaving us, yet I appreciate how emotional pain can slowly kill us. Sometimes I see my self-destructive side as a slow suicide.

Diary Entry: 19.05.09

Sarah and I went hiking up Roseberry Topping on Saturday. It's a big rocky hill in the countryside. Some believe the hill has mystical powers. Maybe it will help me? Sarah and I struggled to the top, huffing, puffing, falling, twisting ankles, pulling muscles and generally feeling like we were going to collapse. At the top we looked at the view and I marvelled with the sight; miles and miles of countryside. I asked Sarah if it made her feel insignificant and if so, did this thought comfort her and put things into perspective? She said yes and asked me if I ever felt like jumping off such a hill and free falling. I agreed that sometimes I will get such an urge but at the moment I am strong enough not to act upon it. I guess I just want to defy physics and prove it can be done. The thought of dying does not scare me, but pain does. However, I am not ready to die yet, I just want help. We went on to discuss my disorder and how it is affecting me. Sarah thinks I may be too self-aware. Maybe she is right. Maybe I spend too much time thinking about borderline and mental illness. But knowledge is power, right? Maybe I do embrace my illness too much because it gives me an identity.

About a week ago Sarah told me that she fears that the devil will come to her in the night. I laughed. The other night I woke up and thought about what Sarah said. I was petrified that the devil was in my room. I guess I was really starting to lose it. I told Sarah. She laughed. As we got in the car to leave Roseberry Topping I turned the keys in the ignition and my mileage counter read 66.6 miles. (The day we discussed the devil on mystical grounds!) We drove a few miles in silence. Crazy? Maybe. We went to the cemetery and placed flowers on May's grave. Sarah is still convinced she was murdered. I don't know. I would rather it be suicide, at least that way she got a choice. I told Sarah that I worry May will appear to me and push me over the edge. Sarah thinks I should worry about Lucifer more! I laughed.

I stayed in bed all day Sunday with the exception of toilet breaks and to get lunch. I could not be bothered with anything. I just didn't have the energy. I looked at my Prozac pillbox left over from my last stint on anti-depressants and thought 'why not take the lot?' Pain over. People would no longer have to put up with me. I could not be arsed to move to the box.

PROZAC

Fluoxetine - 20mg, 40mg, 80mg per day, who cares? When I went to the doctors with low mood these little capsules were prescribed - the miracle cure? Step right up for loss of appetite, loss of sex drive, loss of caring ability, loss of actual treatment. However I must admit that there is usually a slight lift of mood with these little gems. I still feel helpless, but too numb to care. I guess they allow me to see through the fog to focus on the real problem – my illness, whatever it may be.

CHAPTER 6

I plunged my Criminal Law textbook into the bath filled with water and bubble bath to clean it from contamination. I knew I was losing it. I then placed the book on the radiator. I sat in University the next day and sheepishly pulled the book out of my bag. It had expanded to three times it original size, but at least it was clean. I sat in my law class and the defence of insanity was discussed (much more straightforward than sorting out my head). I couldn't concentrate. My hands were contaminated. There was medication everywhere.

"Simply defined Obsessive Compulsive Disorder (OCD) is a lifelong disorder identified by two general groups of symptoms, obsessions and compulsions...Obsessions are intrusive, unwelcome, distressing thoughts and mental images...these thoughts create distress and anxiety... Compulsions are the behaviours that people with OCD perform in a vain attempt to exorcise the fears and anxieties caused by their obsessions." (Schwartz 1996: xiv)

My OCD focuses on the fear of getting pregnant or inadvertently harming someone else. I fear medication will contaminate my contraceptive pill and I will get pregnant and feel the fear that I felt as a child. I worry that medication will somehow be transferred to my hands then end up in my mouth and body. I just have to look at medication and it sends me cold. I never take paracetamol no matter how ill I may feel. The truth is some medications affect the efficiency of the pill and I am not willing to take the risk. I fear just touching medication in case residue is left on my hands. I may place my hands to my lips - then swallow it - then affect my pill - then fall pregnant - not know - drink alcohol -

smoke - harm the unborn - too tired to take the risk. FUCKED UP huh? It makes me feel as I did as a child - helpless. When at University I could not even go into Boots Chemist as the sight of medication made me want to faint. I bought most of my own University textbooks, as I did not know who had touched the library copies. My way of controlling the situation at University was to wash everything I came into contact with that may have (in my mind) been in contact with medication. This included washing bed frames, door handles, mobile phones (one I 'could not get clean' so I put it in the bin), books and shoes. I would spend hours washing. After May's death I referred myself for counseling through my G.P surgery. I told my G.P. that I felt really low and anxious all the time and feared that I would end up like May. I was scared that one day I would lose control and take my own life.

Yvette was the name of the counsellor I visited. She asked me about my previous experiences of counselling and I indulged her. When I told her that I had seen mental health professionals as a child and believed it was because I was sexually abused, her eyes lit up as if all her birthdays had come at once. She then, (practically every session,) would tell me that she was studying a doctorate at University on the effects of sexual abuse on female children. I told her that I thought I was not sexually abused but angry that adults had overreacted. Unlike Maggie she never once challenged my thinking, but instead made a note of it on her writing pad. Probably ticking the denial box on the survey / study she was making me part of. After a few sessions I got fed up of only talking about the sexual side of my problems. I advised her that I was worried about my OCD. I explained that I was constantly worried about contamination and could not get the thoughts out of my head. Such thoughts were making

me anxious, miserable and unable to concentrate on anything else. I told her of my fear of medication and the only tablets I could bring myself to touch were anti-depressants after much reassurance from my G.P that they would not affect my contraceptive pill. I even told her about the constant washing of hands and putting books in the bath. Her response?
'If your house was burning down would you stay in the property to wash you hands?'
'No,' I appropriately responded.
'Then you don't have OCD' she concluded.

As you may know good reader, OCD switches forms. Sometimes it can be fear of contamination and sometimes it can emerge as re-occurring thought ruminations, which make one very anxious all the time. In the example of my house burning down my OCD would probably morph from 'shit my hands are contaminated,' to 'fuck me my family is burning and it must be my fault.' I never saw Yvette again. I went back to my G.P. and asked for another counsellor. The next one was not too bad. She openly admitted that she did not think she could help me and I respected that. Thus I was re-referred to yet another professional. The third was confident that I had OCD but advised that my hand washing and thought ruminations were coping strategies to the anxiety that I felt and therefore were a 'good thing.' In essence she encouraged me to indulge my OCD. Completely fed up, I left counselling and bought a book on OCD and Cognitive Behavioral Therapy (CBT). I taught myself some coping strategies and they help me manage my OCD. Don't get me wrong, some days are better than others but I am still breathing and still coping. I never saw a therapist again until I saw Maggie. I just dosed myself up on Prozac and continued to feel desperate until I could feel desperate no longer.

Flirting With Madness

******

'It's transference' I told Maggie.
'What do you mean?' she asked.
'I transfer all my issues onto Greg to make myself feel better. It's awful, it's abuse,' I cried.
'Greg sounds like an emotionally healthy young man who can look after himself and you are probably being hard on yourself' Maggie replied.
'He is very emotionally balanced, but that does not excuse my actions.' I meekly said.

Maggie and I discussed the word 'shouldn't.' I use it a lot. "Shouldn't' suggests anger Louise.' Maggie said.
'I guess so.' I responded.
I never really knew what to say. Sometimes I did not want to say anything. I just wanted Maggie to wave a magic wand. She never did. The sessions had a routine: 8:45am, before I went to work. I left the house at 8am and drove the 18 miles to Maggie's house. I arrived about 8:35am and waited in the car until 8:42am. Then I knocked on her door. I told myself at the beginning of every session I would not cry. I usually bawled my eyes out.

'Tell me about your brother, Phillip' Maggie asked.
'He is the only one I have never got angry with' I replied.
I wish I were mentally well, so I had the energy to spend more time with him. I am just too self absorbed at the moment and find it hard to deal with anybody else's problems. I want to get better and be the sister he deserves to have. He is 32 years old soon and every year he matures and fights his disability. One of the earliest memories of my brother is seeing him laid on a hospital bed after yet another invasive operation on his

ears when he was a teenager. He had a form of cancer that ate away the bones in his ears. I witnessed my mother and father upset and looking like the world would end whilst trying to put on a brave face for me. Phillip would come to from his operations screaming in pain. Sometimes I believe that if God does exist He really is testing my family who deserve much more luck, as they are good, honest and caring people. For example, my parent's unconditional commitment to Phillip is something I will always admire and cherish.

CHAPTER 7

I was so upset. My life felt like it was spinning out of control. I felt so empty. I did not want to tell Greg as he was going to America for a couple of months travelling. I didn't want to make him feel guilty (despite some of the awful things I said). I knew deep down he was not leaving me, but I couldn't help the way I felt. I felt desperate and crazy. I was being abandoned.

I went walking in the woods / park nearby to where I live and packed in my backpack a bottle of red wine. I found a quiet spot off a footpath that was secluded by trees and a beck. I sat down on a fallen tree trunk and commenced drinking the wine. I got drunk and started to cry. I was content sitting there with my misery. It felt like I deserved it. A woman was walking her dogs along the nearing footpath and she heard me. She shouted to me and asked if I was okay? I shouted back that I was and asked her to leave me alone. She did and I continued to sit and cry whilst it started to rain. Intoxicated, I sat for a while listening to the gentle pattering of the rain against the trees. I staggered home and locked myself in my bedroom. There, I cried myself to sleep.

Eventually my alcohol consumption escalated until I was drinking every night in my bedroom. My objective was to get beyond intoxication into oblivion. As I did not want my parents and Greg to know the quantity of my consumption I hid all the empty liquor bottles under my bed, in my wardrobe, in the loft and in the boot of my car until I could get rid of them secretly. I recall once driving to a local park and waiting until it was quiet so I could put the bottles in the bin without folk noticing. (I was aware that they would make a rather loud clanking noise when they fell into the bin.) When I thought the coast was clear I put the bottles in the park bin only to turn around and see a lady looking straight at me with a look of pity on her face as I heard the bottles clank to the bottom of the bin. I quickly ran back to the car in floods of tears and drove away.

******

'You have a lot of anger built up,' Maggie pointed out.
'Yes, I suppose,' I said.
'It's a hard emotion to shake and it's an exhausting one, Louise.'
Maggie picked up her clipboard and commenced drawing images that depicted my life and emotions. She was very visual. I did not understand this. Black and white words, beautiful black and white words. Who did she think she was? Picasso? I wondered what it was like to be Maggie? I was intrigued. Is she married? She seemed devoted to a higher power as I noticed that she wore a crucifix. (I am yet to figure out what higher power I believe in. My beliefs are a cross between Church of England and Buddhism despite being a Christened Catholic.) Maggie appeared to be a woman of faith who wanted to help others. No wonder she seemed happy, that must be very satisfying. I always thought she was professional but compassionate. I liked her, even if the balance of power was with her.

That night after my anger session with Maggie I spent time staring at the tear in the red paper lining my bedroom wall. That was where I threw my phone against the wall after I picked an argument with Greg. I feared that he had slept with someone else when he was travelling in America. I got the idea from him talking to a female on Facebook, a female who has travelled the world, a person like Greg and not a mental health

sufferer like me. I restarted the fight again the next day whilst at work.
'I couldn't blame you' I screamed down the telephone. 'She is beautiful and I am a fucked up freak.' I was sat in my car, parked up in a deprived council estate which houses many of my clients. People walked past and looked at me like I was crazy whilst I screamed into my mobile phone. I was screaming that I no longer trusted him, as he appeared too friendly with this girl. I accused him of making a fool out of me. I heard him sigh. He was tired of my irrational behaviour. I screamed that all men are the same and why should he not hurt me? Greg clocked that something was wrong. He asked me to elaborate.
'You wanna know my dirty fucking secret' I said. ' I was sexually abused.'
Things went quiet for a while. 'I now understand' he said. 'I love you. I wish you had told me sooner.'

I was crying uncontrollably. I thought about being watched by the twins at 6 years old. I was annoyed that I had allowed that day to harm me so much. I hated myself for holding Greg back. Beautiful, loving Greg, he went from being the point of my anger to being on the pedestal of perfection. I felt stupid. 'I'm damaged goods,' I bawled. I left the conversation to go back to work. I managed to convince my work colleagues that I had hay fever and that was why my eyes were puffy. I was so embarrassed. To this day Greg has supported me and stuck by me. Why do I put him through it? I tell myself he deserves the real me, the nice me. I never thought of myself as angry until I started therapy, but I am. I get angry at everything; phone calls during 'Eastenders,' the dogs whining for a walk, work colleagues acting arrogant, the boy who 'touched' me whilst letting his mates watch, my boss, my friends - the list is endless. It makes me so tired. I am such a bad tempered individual. Don't get me wrong; I am getting better after therapy. Maggie made me more aware of my anger and persuaded me to make a conscious effort to control it. Changes such as not using the word 'shouldn't', taking deep breaths and distracting myself when I am ready to blow. During fits of anger I punch pillows, throw objects at walls and sometimes scream at the top of my voice. Screaming in the car is amusing. Those who witness me driving on the other side of the road appear so shocked and horrified - that makes me laugh.

Diary Entry: 25.05.09

I don't have a lot to write but it needs noting that today I showed my first act of maturity. I apologised to Greg for everything that I have put him through. He seemed so touched by the apology - it made him happy. It was nice to make him happy. I feel I have turned a corner.

P.S. As I write my hair is purple.

Diary Entry: 29.05.09 - 11:59pm.

I am a little drunk and it's nearly Saturday. I have been drinking vodka and I feel depressed. If I am honest I am starting to feel that life is boring again and I am contemplating if there is more to it. Is my life just going to be one big mortgage payment? I want to live a life less ordinary; artistic and sought after. If I don't achieve this, does that make my life void? I HATE myself for thinking like this. I have a good job, a family, and a boyfriend and surely such thoughts are disrespectful. I sometimes feel like I am watching my life rather than living it. Sometimes I wake up and need to 'double take' as I realise I am alive. I am actually here. I question if my experience is reality or simply my perception. When

I studied Philosophy at college we discussed the prospect of infinity and immortality. I was horrified and scared. Surely everything has a beginning and an end. How can I get my head around anything otherwise? I think about how a borderline would cope with the afterlife - no end to anything. In the words of Maggie - 'wow.'

Diary Entry: 30.05.09

Today was weird. I woke up in a foul mood. I was more tired than when I went to bed. Greg and I had planned to go to 'Fountains Abbey' today, yet when I woke up I could not be bothered. I dragged myself into the shower and we set off. I just wanted to cry all the way there. However by mid-afternoon I felt fantastic - 'yo yo Ellison.' We took pictures of our day - God I looked so fat. I have a triple chin. I just want to starve myself.

I'm 24 on Thursday and I still feel lost. I am wasting my life. I have never done anything exciting or memorable. If I were to die tomorrow my obituary would be crap. To quote Hilary Swank in the movie, 'Boys Don't Cry,'

'I have spent most of my life bored.'

Diary Entry: 18.06.09

Decided to go back on anti-depressants today. I have two boxes left over from when I stopped taking them the last time. I want to get better. I mean it. I need to grow up; I finally feel ready. At 8:45am I arrived at Maggie's. I worried that this may be my last session. I don't know why, we have not even discussed termination. Maybe Maggie thinks I am better; she will leave me to cope on my own then I will never get better.

For the first time since my journey began I want to get better. If I am honest part of me hangs onto a label, as an image, as a purpose. It validates me, it makes me interesting and it gets me attention. On Monday night I realised I don't want to live like this any more. I realised that it has been ages since I have cut my skin with scissors or even had the urge to. Recovery is weird. You spend ages thinking therapy is useless, thinking 'I am never going to get better,' then the next day you wake up and realise the progress you have actually made. It smacks you in the face - 6:30pm in the middle of tea. I am improving. I am getting better. I do have a choice, sink or swim? Grow or remain a child? Embrace life or self-sabotage recovery for attention? I choose recovery.

Diary Entry 19.06.09

I just couldn't take it any more. I walked out of the house and started running. I ran along a cycle track at the side of a three-way carriage 'A' road. Bawling and crying, I just wanted the pain to go away. The only thing that seemed to comfort me was the darkness of the night. It was like the darkness was coating me, protecting me, making me invisible. I love dark nights; they are so comforting and romantic. After an hour of running I returned home. I checked my mobile and nobody had called. Surely someone must know I am upset? I felt lonely and overwhelmed. I slid under the duvet and cried myself to sleep.

CHAPTER 8

'Would you like a glass of water?' Maggie asked.
'No.' I looked around the room.
'So how are you?' she questioned.
'I'm good actually, better than I have been for a long time. I feel more motivated. I went back on my anti-depressants.'
'Why?' she asked.
'I want to get better and I can't do that with depression overshadowing my progress and motivation. The signs are back - no energy, no sleep, low mood and anger. I want to be a nicer person but I constantly crave attention' I said.
'That's spoilt child mode Louise. You have had a lot to deal with, you grew up fast and it's not surprising you feel the need for attention. You want to be looked after. Louise, you experienced some bad things as a child, you are craving the 'normal' childhood you felt you never had and now can't have. It's understandable, but you need to leave all the pain and anger in the past' Maggie urged.
'I have tried and I can't' I meekly responded.
'Yes you can, it's going to be hard, but you can do it' Maggie said.
'I suppose.' I said this a lot. 'I just can't get past this self loathing.'
'Wow, self-loathing? How do you think I respond to that? How would you feel if one of the young people you work with said that?' Maggie asked.
'I would be sad' I answered.
'Because you know it's such a strong thing to say. 'Hate' is in the moment. 'Hate' one can move on from quickly, but loathing suggests you are constantly carrying it with you' Maggie informed me. 'Do you think your loved ones want you to feel this way?'

'No - they love me' I told Maggie.
'What don't you like about yourself?' I sensed a challenging tone from Maggie.
'I'm bitchy, I'm moody, I like being alone all the time, I'm short tempered, and I'm two faced and sometimes judgmental' I listed.
'So you are childish? You go into child mode, that child who suffered is acting out and is angry' Maggie stated.
Of course she is acting out!! She was abused, bullied and her family had all the shit luck in the world. Yes she has the right to fucking act out.
'I suppose' I spat.
'That child suffered but you are a young woman and you need to start acting that way Louise. Most of all you need to embrace your life and start living. You are not a bad person. You don't need to self loathe,' Maggie concluded.

There was a silence and I wanted to cry. I kept pinching the top of my legs when Maggie was not looking to distract myself.
'When did the feelings of self loathing start?' Maggie asked.
'When I was about 8,' I replied. 'But it got really bad when I turned 15.'
'How did you cope?'
'I drank alcohol.'
'Did you self harm?' Maggie asked.
'Not really; the odd superficial cut but nothing that scarred, so I guess it was not serious,' I said.
'On the contrary, your scars are different - inside - still serious' Maggie stated.
'I suppose.' (I should have just brought a parrot to answer for me).
'So how are you going to work on what you don't like about yourself?'
'Don't do it as much, I suppose.'

'Elaborate,' Maggie prompted.
'Well, I mean start doing it less. Now that I am more self-aware I can try and limit the bitching and temper etc bit by bit. But it is not going to be easy for me,' I responded.
'Yes but you seem ready to try. You have a lot to do, Louise. We have covered a lot this session. Let's meet next week,' Maggie concluded.

Diary Entry: 21.06.09

Well, I am drunk again. I did well all week. I even went to a gig last night and managed not to drink. All week with no alcohol and today a full bottle of wine and a bottle of port. I am currently sat on my bedroom floor thinking about death. What's it like to die? Ironically it make me realise I am alive and want to live. Tonight is just a relapse, right? I am still getting better, I know it. I'm sick of living inside my head now. The Prozac is making me feel numb. I know it's just until I get used to it again but it doesn't make things any easier. My sex drive has disappeared. Poor Greg - he puts up with a lot and he does not moan. I certainly love him. Anxiety. My chest keeps going tight, like it's going to burst in anticipation.

******

'Take a seat Louise,' Maggie said. I sat down and looked around the room. I looked at the clock on the DVD player in her room; 8:45am. I was bang on time. For a brief second I felt very smug.
'How have you been?' Maggie asked.
'OK, I just feel numb, the tablets are making me feel weird,' I replied.
We spoke again about worrying about the future and things that may not even happen. But most importantly

we discussed my feelings of being a fraud.
'I'm always waiting to be found out,' I said.
'Go on' Maggie prompted.
'Like at work, I'm waiting to be found out, I'm waiting for people to realize that I am rubbish at my job and that I have been fooling them and myself for the past 18 months. Or that those who love me will find out that I am an awful person – a nutter,' I said.
'So you are a fantastic con merchant?' Maggie questioned.
I was shocked, I had never thought of myself as a con artist.
'You're that good that no professional you have worked with is yet to catch you out?' Maggie challenged.
'Well, no,' I meekly replied.
'So you are not a fraud?' Maggie again challenged.
'I suppose not, but I feel that way' I said.
'Wow,' Maggie stated, 'I can see that 'fraud' stamp starting to fade from your forehead. Let it go. Feels good, doesn't it?'
'I suppose,' I predictably ended the session.

******

Diary Entry 27.06.09

Had an awful day today, I felt lethargic and barely made it out of bed. I know the tablets are affecting me, especially my appetite. Not that I am too bothered about that side affect. I feel so fat I need to lose weight. I have had a headache all day. I've had thoughts of suicide again and self harm, but I didn't cut and I don't want to end my life, I just think about it.

Diary Entry 29.06.09

Feel a lot better today. Yesterday was shit. I hardly got

out of bed again. I also got drunk again – Port, Vodka and Cider – I felt like shite. I just lay in bed in front of the TV feeling bored and empty. I self harmed for the first time in ages. Very superficial – I still don't have the guts to press down hard. Nevertheless I was so disappointed with myself when I awoke this morning.

I gave evidence in Crown Court today as a professional witness. I had to laugh to myself; I left the Court looking so respectable. I stood there in the dock and gave my evidence as an expert witness for the barristers and his Honorable Recorder.

I have felt okay today but I have been asking myself why I am so up and down. I hope the tablets will kick in soon. Greg asked if I was okay today, saying that I have been subdued of late. I have, he is right, but hopefully I can maintain today's better mood. My OCD has flared up since I started therapy for BPD. I guess I am opening up my thought processes and the challenge is making me anxious. The only thing is I seem to have developed twitches to my head. Every so often throughout the day I can feel tension building up in my head and then it will twitch two or three times like a tic. I am beginning to learn how to disguise such tic manifestations, especially at work. I feel the tension building and I pretend to rub my neck or I find an excuse and leave my office for a couple of minutes. I am such a freak.

I read this quote today and I rather like it.

"It is as if my life were magically run by two electric currents; joyous positive and despairing negative – which ever is running at the moment dominates my life and floods it.' SYLVIA PLATH (as citied in Keisman and Straus, 2004: 177)

CHAPTER 9

Bars everywhere, the noise, the chaos and the institution. It seemed to suit me. At 21 years old my mates would be moaning about working with snotty customers in shops, University life or standing in the dole queue. I talked about prison, my job in the Prison Service. 'A life less ordinary,' they call it. I enjoyed my time there. It was hard and frustrating but I actually felt accepted in a strange way. I liked working with the offenders, each with their own story to tell and their own journey to travel. Politicians and the media dehumanises them, make them statistics. I guess on some level I related to them, outcast from mainstream society. OCD plagued my time in the Prison Service, although I hid my condition well from my colleagues. I was constantly checking if I had locked the gates and doors, I triple checked everything. In addition, every day I turned up to the gate lodge armed with bacteria hand wash in case I caught some awful disease and passed it on to my loved ones.

Blood was awful. Offenders would fight and attack each other, leaving pools of blood on the cell floors or landing corridors. Only specially trained staff or offenders who are trained are permitted to clean up the blood. Often I would see blood and be required to wait for what felt like an eternity before it went away, before it was cleaned up. I was always on the look out for blood. I was convinced that I would somehow contract HIV and pass it on to Greg. The fear got so bad sometimes that I would avoid sex. If I saw a red substance anywhere I was convinced it was blood and I would have to distance myself from the red substance by at least a metre radius in case I accidentally touched it or got an uncontrollable urge to touch it. Every day for over three years in the Service I went through this.

I started work for the Prison Service in visits in a local male prison. I was based in the Visitor's Centre and looked after the visitors to the establishment. At the end of the shift it was the staff's job to go and lock up the visitors' toilets. I was petrified. Needles and syringes were often found, and in the end I avoided this task and indeed avoided using the toilets. I couldn't catch HIV. Once I was processing a Visiting Order (V.O.) when I noticed dried blood on it. I panicked that I had contracted HIV. I made a doctor's appointment and requested a screening from my G.P. immediately. He convinced me that I did not need a screening and that it was my OCD. I left the surgery feeling like a prick (no pun intended).

One has to be alert at all times in the Prison Service as incidents do happen and folk do get hurt. The environment is a pressure pot. One time I was in one of the Resettlement classrooms talking to one of the officers about how the classes were running. The officer was upset as she did not feel that the department had enough officers on Rota that day. The day was hot and the offenders were being more difficult than usual. Whilst talking with the officer the alarm bell rang and the red lights on the ceiling flashed. The officer leapt into action. Two offenders were fighting in one of the classrooms and the fight soon spilled over to another classroom and more offenders got involved. In the end our very stressed officer locked all the classroom doors to prevent any more offenders getting involved with the ongoing fights. For safety reasons I made the decision to lock the office that I was in to prevent offenders getting inside as the office housed in its drawers scissors and confidential security information. In the scuffle I ended up locked in the office with two offenders. I should have been worried for my safety but fortunately I was trapped with two non-violent offenders. One of them was the campest lad that I had ever met. He kept telling me how he wanted to be a hairdresser and how unfashionable the prison uniforms were. I had to laugh. Human diversity is brilliant.

In between being an anxious wreck and a triple checker I performed well in the Prison Service and at 22 years of age I was promoted to management level and given the responsibility of managing staff, rotas and even some budgets. On the outside I was an ambitious graduate with great potential, yet on the inside I did not have a clue what I was doing with my life or if I was even sane. My managers tried to convince me to apply for a graduate fast track scheme with the aim of becoming a Governor grade in the future. I did not apply, not because my ambition didn't tell me to, but because I was scared of being trapped in a job, of being trapped with responsibility for others. Thus I let the opportunity slip through my fingers. My managers were disappointed, but what was I meant to do? Tell the truth on my application? Never be able to find a job again? Have people think I am crazy? No fucking way.

Diary Entry 04.07.09

I feel really shit at the moment. I feel I need to be re-born as someone else. I don't know what I want out of life and am feeling very desperate. I thought again about suicide this morning, not seriously but in passing. I was fantasising that I had taken an overdose and my boyfriend, friends and family were looking after me afterwards. They finally knew the pain I was going through. They were helping me, loving this horrible defected being. Then I felt guilty; what sort of manipulative bitch am I? I guess I just want to tell those close to me my real pain. I can't cope with this front any more.

I just want to be alone at the moment. I don't want to see people. The whole thought of having to act happy makes me want to cry. I just want to lock myself up and get drunk or high. I haven't smoked cannabis in ages and I wish I had some right now. I want to be out of it, to be in oblivion. I want to go wild. I have spent practically all day lying in bed drinking Jack Daniels. Writing this entry is all I have really done. I hate living in this town. I want to live in a city, any city – just some life. I hate feeling so trapped in run down suburbia. My other wish is to be cuddled and held. I feel so lonely. I know it's my fault. I avoid people. I'm just so scared to ask Greg to just hold me for hours, but I really want it, I really need it. I need to let my guard down.

Diary Entry 05.07.09

Went to Greg's niece's christening today. It was lovely and everyone had a great time, even me, but I couldn't help feeling like I didn't belong. Everyone was enjoying themselves and each other's company. All was so normal. I sat there feeling like a freak. Then I looked at Greg and thought why are you with me? Why not find a normal girl, a girl who knows how to be satisfied and not a girl who doesn't even know who she is? I have been thinking this a lot lately; who am I? I really don't know. All I know is I am not the girl I am at the moment.

Whilst drunk last night I was lying down on the bed and suddenly shouted out May's name. I wanted to talk to her, ask her how she felt before she died. No response. I guess I was desperate. I just need somebody to understand how I am feeling. There is a big part of me that wants to share my feelings with Greg, my mother and my father, but another part of me cannot bear the thought of burdening them, as I love them so much. I feel so lonely. That's when I think about suicide. If I succeed then the pain is over. If I don't then I will be made to tell others. I hate myself for being this manipulative.

I see Maggie again on Wednesday and part of me can't wait. I feel so low. I am starting to doubt whether I will ever get better; all that money on therapy for nothing. Maybe at 24 years old my thoughts are just too entrenched? Maybe this is my fate. Maybe I should be alone and stop hurting the ones I love. I constantly want to be alone. I know it is not good for me, but I am scared of breaking down. It's easier to lock myself away in my bedroom.

******

Finally it was Wednesday, 8:45am, bang on time again.
'Come in Louise, take a seat. I'll just fetch some water. Would you like some?' Maggie greeted me.
'No thanks.'
'Right Louise, you have been coming to see me for a while now; we need to do a review of your progress' Maggie told me. Oh great, I thought, she is going to determine I am as well as I can be and refuse to meet with me any more. I worried I was going to be abandoned. We discussed therapy to date and Maggie asked if there had been any benefit.
'Yes, I don't feel as bad as I did, but I still feel so empty' I told her.
'Okay, let's discuss that today then. Explain to me what you mean by empty?'
'I just feel numb and neither here nor there. This happens more so when my depression lifts. Sometimes I would rather be depressed; at least then I would know

that I have the capacity to feel, I would know that I exist and am alive' I answered.
'When do you feel most empty?' Maggie prompted.
'Weekends. When I am not at work. I'm not saying work makes me content, but it distracts me I suppose. However, I can't bear the thought of having to be a workaholic just to avoid emptiness' I moped.
'So what can you do on a weekend to avoid the emptiness?'
'I don't know' I pathetically responded.
'Yes you do. I don't mean to keep challenging you Louise, but the answers are there in you.'
'Well, I feel good when I am being creative, especially when I write. I feel some purpose' I admitted.
'Why not write a book?' Maggie asked.
'I am, I just have writer's block, and I feel so disconnected.'
'Is the book dark?'
'Yes.'
'Okay, what else can fill your emptiness?' Maggie challenged.
'Relationships, but I feel so low that I don't seem to have the energy to invest. I can't let my guard down' I replied.
'What about your relationship with Greg, what is that like?' Maggie enquired.
'It's good, but my mood is taking the fun out of everything.'
'Then it needs more fun, fun that only you can bring' Maggie concluded.
'I suppose.'
'Are you honest with Greg?'
'Most of the time, yes.'
'What are you not honest about?'
'My feelings' I said.
'So you don't feel that intimate?' Maggie summarised.
'I guess not, no' I concluded. I thought about this

statement, that question, and I was shocked. I had always thought I was intimate with Greg. I guess I had never been fully intimate with anyone. I always felt the need to put on an act. I had not even been intimate with myself.
'Is there anyone you are honest with?' Maggie asked.
'Not really; I tell Sarah my friend a lot.'
'So you find intimacy easier with friendships?'
'Yes, I would agree with that' I said. 'I don't worry about Sarah's reaction. I know she will be there no matter what. I could do something awful like murder someone and she would still stand by me and me by her.'
'So why are you not like this with Greg?' Maggie questioned.
'I want to be, but I am scared. Sarah is very like me. She understands my pain. She suffers the same thoughts and feelings as I do. Greg may be really shocked. He may get to know the real me, and run away. I don't feel strong enough to take the risk' I said.
'Or maybe he will support you and help you get better? You have to let him in to do that,' Maggie informed me.

I started to cry. I was angry; I had promised myself no more crying in these sessions. Maggie handed me a tissue. She looked sad. I felt like a bad pupil. I felt like a disappointment.
'It's easier for me to be alone when I feel like this. I know it is not healthy or helping me but it is easier. I just lock myself up in my room and miss family events and everything. I know it really hurts Greg when I make excuses to not attend family occasions. I hate hurting him,' I told Maggie.
'Why do you avoid them then?'
'I feel on display, I feel judged I suppose, which is awful since his family have never judged me,' I said.
'You talk about being on display, about being judged, it would appear that you have a 'me and them' attitude.

It's like you versus the world. Would you agree?' Maggie asked.

'I suppose.' (I was like a broken record, I know.)

'So you handle it by isolating yourself?' Maggie questioned.

'I do it to protect myself. If I don't let anybody in, I can't be hurt and I can't be vulnerable' I quickly interjected.

'Exactly, but isolation just fuels your feelings of being lonely, which leads to emptiness, which in turn leads to the dissociation of 'me and them.' Do you see? You are crossing the borders' Maggie advised.

'Yes, but I can't fix it overnight,' I felt myself snapping.

'No I realise that, but small steps are needed. Try and improve your relationships one at a time. Get to know people again. Stop categorising them; is this something you can do?'

'Yes, but slowly' I replied.

'Maybe then your writer's block may clear a bit' Maggie optimistically stated.

'I hope so, I would love to write, but maybe I should grow up and stop wishing on a pipe dream,' I said.

'Louise, writing a book is hard, it takes dedication. I think it is very adult to stick to it,' Maggie advised.

'I will,' I concluded the session.

Diary Entry 08.07.09

I left Maggie's today absolutely knackered. Mascara was running down my face and I had to rush straight to work. Ironically after leaving Maggie's I went to visit one of my clients and had to spend the rest of the morning trying to get my client to see his self worth. He suffers from Conduct Disorder.

Work was okay. I felt in adequate spirits when I finally got back to the office at lunchtime. I tried to think about what Maggie had said, about not always having a guard up. I laughed and joked with my work mates and overall had an okay day.

Greg emailed me at work and asked how my session with Maggie had gone. I told him a little bit, careful not to disclose everything. Then it hit me. Maggie was right, I was keeping him at arm's length. I was shutting him out again. I emailed him back and told him about what Maggie and I discussed about not being as honest with him as I could be. He agreed. He also stated that my honesty is likely to bring us closer together. I told him I am scared that telling him everything would make him 'run for the hills.' Then out of nowhere I emailed him and told him that I self harm. Great I told him in an email – very intimate!!! He responded. He was concerned. He did not run. Maybe I really should give this intimacy thing a go.

I have been at Greg's all evening. He has been busy doing his university work so I have been on the P.C. I have updated my Facebook page. Hopefully I can start working on some of those relationships I have let slide. I go to London in a week and a bit and I can't bloody wait. Noise, lights and city life, what more could one want? Surely I can't be bored and empty there?

Dairy Entry: 11.07.09

I don't feel too good today. I feel down and sad. I'm having trouble sleeping again. I keep waking up at 3am, which I find disturbing since that is the demonic hour. Maybe it's symbolic of the demons I have to fight every day in my head.

I was drunk again last night. Alone drinking white wine. I can't remember going to bed or what time I crashed so I guess I was pretty out of it. I feel like utter crap for allowing the booze to creep up on me again, but I also don't feel able to cope any other way right now. I keep thinking about what Maggie said to me about intimacy. I have struggled with this nearly all my life. I have always worried that people will find out the real me is a fucking loony. I guess at times I am, but I don't have the strength at the moment to deal with the stigma. Yesterday, I phoned up to activate my credit card and the 'advisor' on the end of the line persuaded me to take out insurance in case I lose my job. HOWEVER this cover excludes losing your job through a mental illness. Are we not as ill as someone who has broken an arm or who is suffering a bad disease? Don't we all just need support and time and help to heal?

I'm still lying in bed. I don't see much point in getting up, to be honest. I feel bored, tired and empty. I would rather be asleep and wake up to a better day, some other time. I am starting to think that maybe life is just going through the motions and certain individuals deal with the 'groundhog' existence better. Either that or they don't see life for what it really is.

Diary Entry 12.07.09 pt 1

Feeling a lot better today. I think it is because I woke up next to Greg. I feel like I am falling in love all over again. I've put him through so much lately and he is still standing by me. Last night we made love for the first time in weeks. It was great. For the first time in ages I felt close to him again. I need to get better for us. I need to give him the girlfriend he deserves.

Diary Entry 12.07.09 pt2

Just watched the film 'Pollock.' It's a movie about Jackson Pollock, the American abstract artist who hit fame in New York in the 1940s and 1950s. Speculation indicates that he suffered BPD. I must say the film did portray this. He was such a tortured soul. Creative but full of self-doubt and mood instability. He also suffered alcoholism, which in the end killed him. He crashed his car drunk. Makes one realise how serious mental illness really is. We are not attention seekers. We are potentially committing a long drawn out suicide.

I'll be going to bed soon. I have to give evidence in Court tomorrow. At least the press won't be there this time as it is a closed Court. Last time I ended up in the local paper described as a 'professional' witness – FAME.

Diary Entry 13.07.09

We won the Court case!!!!!

CHAPTER 10

Sorry good readers for now discussing my squidgey parts, but less than two years ago I faced a breast cancer scare. I had a tumour in my right breast. It is not related to my mental health I know, but I am including it in this literature as an example of how mental illness is STILL stigmatised in the work place. The relevance will become evident as your read.

I have always suffered lumpy breasts and when I discovered a lump in my right breast I was not too worried. Nevertheless, to pacify my boyfriend and my mother, and to calm what could potentially fuel my OCD into thinking I was dying or had AIDS, I went to a doctor who referred me to the local hospital. The doctor told me that she thought my lump was a cyst and the hospital appointment would be a formality. When I arrived at the hospital I saw a consultant who coldly told me that I did not have a cyst but a tumour. Not only did the examination leave me feeling vulnerable and slightly violated, I had to digest that news. He advised that a biopsy would be needed to determine if the tumour was cancerous or benign. After the biopsy I broke down over my mother in the hospital. I told my mother that I felt like a piece of meat rushed through a procedure with no consideration at all. I felt vulnerable and powerless.

Upon returning home the anaesthetic wore off from the biopsy and I was in much more pain than I had anticipated. I was in agony. I of course can't take painkillers as they may affect my contraceptive pill, so I dealt with the pain with no medication. I started to think about the possibility of having cancer and possibly needing surgery. A small part of me was scared but another part of me fantasised about being looked after, about having a break in hospital from all the responsibility of life. I mean who could hate or expect anything from a cancer victim? I summarised that if I had cancer and survived then I would be a stronger person for it. If I had cancer and died, then at least this emotional pain would be over. I told this to Deborah, my boss from the Prison Service. She is someone I trust very much and someone I have remained close to over the years. Deborah immediately wanted to meet with me. When we met she hugged me and told me I needed help. I agreed.

I did not know anything about BPD when the incident occurred. All I knew was that I was constantly worrying about everything, felt empty, alone, was drinking alcohol regularly and very uncomfortable with who I was. I started to feel very depressed and the tumour was just the last straw for me. I found myself worn out and downtrodden. Going to work felt like I was climbing Everest. I made the decision that I needed a rest; the tumour was a wake up call. I needed to re-charge. I went to the doctors and my G.P. agreed that with the tumour and depressive feelings I was having I needed a rest. I was signed off work for two weeks and prescribed anti-depressants. Whereas I was honest with my managers in the Prison Service regarding my mental health, I was not so forthcoming with my then manager. The prison never judged me, as they knew I did an excellent job and my performance reflected that. In fact one senior manager told me that they thought more of me because I had academic and management ability with the troubles I had.

My manager seemed supportive at first. She told me that my work spoke for itself, that I was one of the best members of staff she had and we all needed a break sometimes. I thanked her and even wrote Court reports from home whilst on sick leave to save her getting the work re-allocated. After a week or so I started to feel better. I was rested, had got some sleep and was coming to terms with the waiting game of the tumour diagnosis. I felt well enough to put my mask back on and go back to work when my sick note expired. It was about this time that I received a call from Human Resources. They needed me to attend an interview with occupational health to determine my capability to do my job. I was furious. I explained to the brash adviser on the telephone (who spoke to me like a child,) that my sick note covered me for another week and that such an interview would have to wait. 'No Miss, you have to come to the interview before returning to work' she said smugly. At that I put down the phone and called my manager. 'It's a formality,' she said. ' I have no worries about you. Don't be mad.'

I turned up to the meeting still feeling angry. I sat in the waiting room of the occupational health provider and noticed a sign that stated, 'Please do not consume the beverages if here for a drugs or alcohol test.' A nurse called me into her office. She told me that my sickness was unacceptable and challenged that perhaps I should quit my job due to 'stress.'
'I managed two departments in a prison in my early 20s and improved nearly all the performance targets with my contribution. How dare you think that it is the job which is causing me 'stress', you know nothing about me. I actually love my job and I feel good and efficient at work. The reason I took this 'rest' was so I could give full commitment to my clients. How dare you make assumptions? I would like to see how you would feel not knowing if a tumour in your breast was cancerous' I spat.
'Pardon. Tumour?' she asked.
'Yes, the main reason why I feel so shit' I told her. 'My

mood does not affect my ability' I said.
'It says nothing about that in the referral from you manager, just that she worries your depression makes you incompetent' she informed me.

Needless to say I told my manager what I thought of her referral and informed her of the Disability Discrimination Act. Yes, mental illness is a hard illness to live with, but it does not always impact on one's ability to fulfil job descriptions. Employers have no right to treat people this way. I signed myself back to work early and made sure that my manager commented on the HR form it was because of the victimisation I felt. I also noted that in the seven years I have been working (including working in a pressure pot prison), this period of absence was isolated and after I had undergone a biopsy. I made it clear that a repeat of such treatment would be taken to a higher level. It is amazing, the occupational health report went 'missing' and I was not formally placed on sickness monitoring procedures.

******

Diary entry 15.07.09

Absolutely knackered today. I can't remember going to bed last night and I woke up with bruises all over my body. I dreamt last night that I was in a small swimming pool alone with the exception of three women laughing at me. I was yearning to enter the 'big pool' that I could visibly see from where I was treading water. I was struggling to get to the 'big pool' where hundreds of other people were. To get there I had to battle a thrashing river with a strong current. Just as I was about to win my fight the Police stopped me. I then woke up. I have read that in dreams water symbolises life. I guess I want a better life, a bigger life, but my emotional waves and my relationship with authority keeps stopping me.

I gave a presentation at work this afternoon on two successful cases that I have managed and how my once risky clients are leading productive lives. I presented to my team the importance of not giving up on people. Irony? I think so.

Diary entry 16.07.09

Had a weird day today. My tablets seem to be finally kicking in. Don't get me wrong, I still feel empty and bored most of the time, but I don't feel as 'depressed'. I just feel frustrated. I am pissed off that I am ill. I just want to feel normality, not to be normal but to feel it. I self harmed again yesterday. I felt a certain satisfaction seeing the blood at the top of my thighs. I had the guts to press down this time. I told Greg and felt so awful.

Dairy entry 21.07.09

As I write I am sat in a hotel in Central London. Greg and I are staying in Queensway, near to Hyde Park. The hotel is okay, even if there is not enough room to swing a cat. I went to the Tate Gallery of Modern Art today and viewed works by Pollock and Warhol, which were amazing. London is great and I love the city. I honestly believe that travel is a protective factor for me, especially the cities; so much to do, so much culture to distract the brain.

I first travelled at the age of 22 when I visited the big apple with Greg. I was not one bit interested in the New York City of the tourist, as I wanted to see the real New York, the fast paced city where anything can happen and anyone can achieve. New York has a beat, a pulse, which runs through the city. The sounds of the city make an ensemble, hard to forget and shake. The honking of taxi horns, the crashing of trash cans, the hum of the subway - folk shouting in the subway. New York City is its own little world contained in the subway steam, which rises from the underground. The island of Manhattan is certainly one of my protective factors. My favourite district is the Lower East Side and the Bowery, basically the skid row / poor district. However what it lacks in Times Square finance it makes up for in bohemian masterminds and artistic ability. Some of the folk there are just purely crazy – absolutely beautiful.

I recall one evening being bored in a hotel room in Times Square. Greg and I were staying at the Edison Hotel, which is a jazz themed hotel. I was thrilled that I was in the same hotel that Chris Stein of 'Blondie' once lived in in the 1970s. Despite the legend of the hotel there was little to do after dark, with the exception of ordering a predictable pre-paid movie. On this particular night I was bored and told Greg that I wanted to get a drink. Greg was tired and went to bed. I told him that I was going to the hotel bar to get a bevy and that I would only be a short time. I kissed him goodnight and left the hotel room and headed for the bar. When I got to the bar it was like a ghost town. I made the decision to go out into the night to find some fun. I ventured out into Times Square, already intoxicated with a bottle of Jack Daniels that I had bought from Heathrow Airport. I staggered past folk on the sidewalk into the road and nearly fell over a Policeman attempting to direct traffic. I was lucky that the Policeman was too busy checking out four beautiful women on the opposite side of the road. Finally I settled at the Hard Rock Café. At first I felt slightly self-conscious to be drinking alone, but after a couple more Jack Daniels and watching 'Guns 'n'

Roses' on the bar television I soon felt at home. By the end of a serious drinking session and having a dance with two gay Canadians and a pink feather boa I decided to leave the bar.

When I finally made it back to the hotel I promised myself that I would be quiet and not wake Greg. Yet upon seeing my hotel key, which had an advertisement for the musical 'Hairspray,' I suddenly started to sing, 'Good Morning Baltimore' at the top of my voice while trying to open my hotel room door. I don't think the other residents of the hotel or Greg was too happy with my actions. 'I am just acting my age,' I told myself.

One of the best things about being situated in Times Square is the accessibility to Broadway. The biggest shock for me was how small Broadway was. As a misguided European one expects red carpets, limos, not small theatres dotted about the theatre district. However do not be fooled, this only provides a tardis affect. The shows are huge, bold, witty and bright. The music has perfect dynamics and rhythm. The stories on Broadway flow beautifully with a sense of irony. One of my favourite shows I have seen on Broadway is 'Avenue Q.' The theme of the show is, 'what is my purpose?' The musical is told by sex crazed, foul mouthed puppets. I sat watching the show laughing, yet feeling empathy for the lead puppet. He did not know where his place was in this world. I wanted to hug his big head made out of cloth. I can't say that I had such a profound feeling during 'Hairspray,' 'Spamalot' or 'Mary Poppins.' In fact in the latter I feel asleep half way through due to drinking a full bottle of Jack Daniels. (I think I got a better deal than those who stayed awake.)

My favourite district in NYC is the Bowery. I am not too sure if I would survive here after dark, but it screams art and creativity to me. After watching numerous documentaries about New York Punk, I grew up dreaming of having a beer in the music club CBGBs. Unfortunately it closed its doors before I could get my intoxication. I first visited the Bowery in August 2007 and I stood outside what is a shockingly small shell of what used to be the legendary music venue. In my opinion CBGBs is to New York what the Cavern Club is to Liverpool. Skulking outside her closed doors I read the graffiti on the shutters covering what was the front doors. The words sum up the attitude of what was the New York Punk movement. One included, "I saw the best minds of my generation vanish to Vegas Bank, P. Smith". Although my favourite piece of graffiti was, "I wish I was there, but fuck I am only 7," Anon.

Also in the Bowery district is the boutique 'Trash and Vaudeville.' Man, what a store. It is full of punk clothes. Here I bought my favourite jeans – skinny white jeans, patterned with black punk graffiti. (I so wish I could control my binge eating so I could fit into them.) The sad thing about the Bowery however is the amount of homeless folk. It saddens me that people are still living on the streets in the 21st Century. Last time I went to the Bowery there was a homeless man sat outside McDonalds whilst Greg and I ate breakfast there. I couldn't cope with it, so I went outside and gave the man half of my breakfast. However it was not a selfless act, I guess I just felt too guilty for not realising how good my life was.

Recently Greg took me to Paris for Valentine's Day. I certainly understand why it is classed as the romantic capital of the world. The art, architecture and literature are to die for. Paris thrives on culture and therefore I thrived on Paris. Folk take no crap in Paris and if you anger them, it is promptly stated. Also I love Paris as it is socially acceptable to drink alcohol before noon. Throughout my time in Paris I felt a painful desire to lead a creative life. I was sad to think about my current existence. I felt boring, stuck in the 9-5 rat race to break even every month. I felt like I was living a 60-year plus slow death. At Notre Dame there was an opportunity to write a 'silent prayer' and place it in an anonymous box. I wrote on my prayer, 'Please find me, I am lost.' Looking around the Cathedral, so many devout believers were ecstatic to be praying to God. I felt envy. How could they be so sure about what they believed in?

Diary Entry 22.07.09

I feel a wee bit emotional and overwhelmed of late. I let Greg read my diary / writings on Saturday night. He now knows what shite goes on inside my head. He said he loves me and wants to support me through it. This has really helped. I no longer feel totally alone. However, I do worry that I will become reliant on him and it will hurt if he leaves. Worse still, I worry that I will be a burden on him. When in bed earlier I know that he noticed the cuts on my thighs. I have not consumed that much alcohol and I feel good for it. Although Greg did tell me off for having a whiskey at 10am this morning – 'I am on holiday' I told him.

Diary entry 26.07.09

Had an awful day today. I got out of bed at about 11:15am (about 2 hours after Greg left for work) and by 11:30am had started drinking alcohol. I finally stopped at 5:30pm when I fell asleep. Basically I just got drunk and lay in bed watching telly. Also throughout the day I self harmed again. I considered taking all my anti-depressants at once, not to kill myself but for some rest – a cliché cry for help, I suppose. Then I thought about how my loved ones would feel. This stopped me and I opted for whiskey instead. I do feel guilty and I am really beginning to get fed up with myself. I woke up at 7pm and after some water I felt a little better.

CHAPTER 11

'Come on in Louise, take a seat. Would you like some water?' Maggie said, predictable as ever.
'No thank you' I replied.
'How are you?' Maggie opened.
'Fine, I suppose.'
'How's work going?'
'Okay, can't complain.' I remained guarded.

I could sense Maggie was itching for me to give her something to work with.
'So you are totally fine at work then?'
'Sometimes I feel bored, not with my clients though. I like working with them as every day is different and I like helping them as I feel I have some worth. However I get so bored with the paperwork that it is becoming a drag. I sometimes feel like I am stuck in Groundhog Day. Is this life I ask? Everyday the same – waiting to be bored' I told Maggie.
'You use the word bored a lot, Louise.'
'Yes, that's how I feel. If I am not in a situation of high stimuli I feel bored.'
'So life is boring?' Maggie concluded for me.
'9-5 is.'
'So adult life is boring?'
'Yes, yes it is.'
'Do you not think your view is very childish? A 13 year old says everything is boring,' Maggie challenged.
'I know, but I can't help the way I feel, especially in my own private time, I feel bored and empty' I said.
'We keep coming back to this and it's understandable, it's part of what may be borderline, but we need to address it and find something to fill your void.'
' I know' I meekly responded.
'Part of me just wants to put you on a bouncy castle and

give you an afternoon of pure fun to help fill your void. You feel that you missed out as a child on careless fun due to your mental health and you experienced a lot for a person so young, but you must accept you are no longer a little girl. You need to fill your voids with adult fun,' Maggie said.

'I know' I repeated.

'So how do you fill the void feeling at the moment?' Maggie asked.

'I act like a self destructive teenager.'

'Why?'

'Because it makes me less boring. I don't want my obituary to say 'mediocre'. In terms of my self harming it just makes me feel better in the short term' I told her.

'So part of you looks forward to your self destructive side as it validates your wild side?' Maggie asked.

'Yes, I guess so,' I said.

'So what fills the void that does not damage your health?'

'My writing and being with Greg,' I replied.

'How would you react if Greg acted like you?'

'I would stop him, sit on him if I had to,' I said.

'Why?'

'Because he would be hurting himself and be in pain.'

'But it's okay for you to be in pain and harm yourself?' Maggie concluded.

'That's different'

'How?'

'Because to only think about yourself is selfish' I responded.

'Louise, self love is not selfish, it is necessary. You must start loving yourself and taking care of you before anyone else' Maggie said.

As Maggie continued to talk I started to feel dizzy and my eyes struggled to focus. I felt really light headed. I was detaching. I could see Maggie's lips moving but I couldn't ascertain what she was saying. I felt scared that I was going to faint. Everything appeared to be in slow motion. 'Louise, you must start looking after yourself, you have a serious illness. You need to get yourself strong before anything else,' Maggie said as I finally started to hear her words again. I knew Maggie was right and that was why I was sitting in the chair opposite her and paying her an hourly rate.

Diary Entry 03.08.09.

I did a test today on the Internet regarding alcohol. I did three different tests and the results were all the same – that I have alcohol dependency and alcoholism. It shocked me. I have always thought that I choose to drink and because I don't drink in work hours or get in the car intoxicated I was not an alcoholic or a sufferer of alcoholism. I decided NOT to have a drink tonight after tea as I usually would. I struggled. I felt sick, light headed and irritable. I drank tea and water and it felt pathetic to be honest. God, I did not realise how out of control my life is getting.

******

After a week of serious thought I texted Maggie and told her that I wanted a break from our therapy sessions. I felt as though I had gone as far as I could with her for the time being. She texted back, 'fine.' I must admit I was slightly upset that she never tried to convince me to stay in therapy with her, but I understand that she was just being professional and not pushing me. I wrote to my doctor requesting a copy of my mental health records, in particular those relating to my childhood and adolescent years, as I wanted to try and piece together my life by looking at how I got to where I am today. It transpires that such records are now held by the local trust hospital. A clerk from my G.P.'s surgery attempted to telephone me to pass on this information. She phoned three times when I was at work and my mother took the calls. At first my mother thought little of it when the surgery rang. At the third phone call my mother started to worry that something was seriously wrong with me. Of course she is right, mental illness is very serious, but my mother presumed I had a serious physical illness like cancer or HIV. She telephoned me at work and asked me what I was keeping from her.

'I can't talk now,' I said.

'Louise, you need to tell me.'

'Okay, two secs; I will find somewhere quiet, hold on,' I replied. I went into my boss's office as it was free, sat down at her desk and prepared to discuss my mental health with my mother.

'I just wanted a copy of my medical records,' I meekly stated.

'Why? Does your boss want a copy?' my mother asked.

'No, I wanted the copies.'

'Whatever for?' my mother pondered.

'For information,' I responded. I started to cry. I knew I had to tell her about what had been going on in my head.

'I am not well,' I sobbed. 'My mental health is really bad. I've been going to private counselling.'

'What for?' Mother asked.

'I have all the symptoms of Borderline Personality Disorder. It's worse than depression. I don't know who I am and I am struggling to cope. I'm going to lose my job, I know it. I'm going to end up in a hospital. I am really bad, Mum. I have been self harming and thinking about suicide. I am so tired,' I cried.

'Come straight home and we will talk,' my mother ordered.

'I can't, I have to drive to the prison to see a client. It's a 160 mile round trip. I will come home after that.' I said.

Flirting With Madness

'Okay, but you need to start being honest with me. I know you are drinking a lot and locking yourself away in your bedroom. Isolating yourself will not help. Your father and I love you' she said.
'I know, I will see you tonight.' I ended the telephone call.

I put the phone down and ran straight to the toilet. I splashed water on my face and looked in the mirror. I looked an absolute mess. My eyes were puffy and my pale complexion was all red. I wiped the running mascara from my eyes and hid in the toilets for twenty minutes. I then made my way back to my desk to prepare for the prison visit. I emailed Greg at work and asked him to come home with me to help me explain things to my parents. He agreed. After work I picked up Greg and we made our way to my home. Together we entered the living room and sat on the sofa with my parents. I started to cry. I told them everything. I left nothing out. I sat there in my mother's arms for hours afterwards. It was decided that I was not to go into work the next day, but instead I would be going to the doctors.

I awoke the following morning with a headache and feeling more tired than when I went to bed. Mother got me an appointment with the doctor for that morning. It was not with my usual doctor and I was a little nervous about having to explain my mental health to yet another professional. Mother drove the short distance from our home to the surgery. In what seemed like a blur I found myself sat in the surgery waiting room. I felt paranoid that everyone knew I was a head case. I was sat in the waiting room chair fidgeting and feeling dizzy. I felt embarrassed; 24 years old, progressive career, an honours degree, yet I was still unable to function and feel like a 'normal' adult. After thirty minutes of sitting in the waiting room my name was called to see Doctor Smith. I told the doctor about my sessions with Maggie and that I went to private counselling as I feared having BPD on my medical records may make me unemployable.

'Louise, personality disorders are such grey areas in psychiatry. Many still believe that they are untreatable and as such treatment is limited in the UK. I am reluctant to label you' Dr Smith said.

'The counsellor I have been seeing appeared to believe that I was suffering BPD and the treatment did help,' I responded.

'Borderline traits are certainly evident in you and it is a strong possibility that you are suffering the illness. Some people I see are low functioning borderlines and need the diagnosis to receive immediate treatment. However, I believe we should focus on your depression. You are a high functioning individual who may be at a detriment from the diagnosis. Your depression is the priority at the moment' Dr Smith concluded.

I had to fill in a questionnaire regarding my feelings. It is a questionnaire that I have come to know almost rubidium as I have filled in so many over the years. It asks, 'In the past two weeks have you felt suicidal, self harmed, had little energy, felt lonely etc.?' I ticked yes to all of the questions. The prescription of Fluoxetine came next.

'Louise, you must stay on this medication for at least six months after you start to feel better. You have a history of stopping and starting the medication and this is not helping you. I also recommend that you exercise and have a rest from work' Dr Smith advised.

'I can't be off work, they will declare me incompetent and fire me. Last time they told me I would face disciplinary action' I told him.

'It sounds like you have very ignorant employers. What

is your line or work?' Dr Smith asked.

'I work in probation, working with young people,' I said.

'Well it sounds like you are a skilled and intelligent individual. Depression cannot take such skills away from you. You have an illness and we need to find a way to treat it. It is exactly the same as a physical illness that needs attention. If your employer has an issue with your medical competence then tell them to contact me and I will enlighten their ignorance. Did you receive any formal warning for your sick note six months ago?' Dr Smith asked.

'No, I am still yet to receive any feedback from occupational health' I replied.

'What a surprise,' was his sarcastic response.

I smiled slightly. I was glad that I got an appointment with him. He seemed very supportive. He wrote me a sick note for two weeks and told me to make another appointment after a fortnight to assess my response to the medication and review my sick note.

'Also Louise, I think you would benefit from more therapy. Is it okay for me to refer you to one of our surgery counsellors?' Dr Smith asked.

'Yes, as long as it is not Yvette who told me I didn't have OCD' I responded.

'No, I don't think you should see her again either. I was thinking of our Gateway Worker as she has an excellent reputation. She also won't charge you,' Dr Smith grinned.

I smiled and agreed. If angels exist on earth, I think he may certainly be one.

When I arrived home I telephoned work. I could not speak to my manager as she was off sick with stress (how ironic), so I spoke to the acting line manager. I told him I had a sick note for two weeks for 'low mood' and would email him what I needed covering in terms of client contacts. He sounded embarrassed as I requested not be contacted at home whilst on sick leave like on the last occasion.

Diary Entry 17.08.09

I joined the gym last week as the doctor told me I needed to get more exercise into my life. It has been so difficult as my energy levels are at rock bottom and I have had to force myself to go to the gym. I must admit that when I am at the gym I feel better. It is like I am exercising away the cobwebs off my mind. I wish the feeling could last. Since going to the doctor's I have cut back on the booze. Today I poured a bottle of vodka down the sink. I don't want to become an alcoholic. I am certainly alcohol dependent to a certain extent, but I will be damned If I will let alcohol ruin me.

I went camping over the weekend with Sarah. It was ace. It rained heavily with gale force winds. It was so so so funny, lying there in a leaky tent in the middle of a farm in the Lake District. The gale force winds hit the surrounding trees before the tent and made a howling sound like something out of a horror movie. By the morning the farm was waterlogged and we had to admit defeat and pack up in fear of catching a virus. The Sat Nav took us down roads that Sarah described as 'cycle tracks.' The drive was in the middle of and half way up a mountain, thus rather dangerous. I loved it, the adrenaline rush was marvellous, and I felt so alive.

Diary Entry: 24.08.09

I am still off work at the moment. Going to the gym still, but getting very frustrated as I don't seem to be getting any fitter or thinner. I feel so tired it's unbelievable. My sick note runs out in a couple of days and therefore I need to see the doctor again tomorrow. I don't feel ready for work at the moment. I wrote a report today for work and emailed it in.

I still feel in limbo. I can't see past one day to the next out of fear. I keep thinking I will wake up from my life, that this is not really happening to me and that it's someone else's reality that I am perceiving. I am trying to be positive. I am reading more spiritual books and I am trying to embrace the power of positive thought and energy but it's very hard when you need to pop Prozac every day. My friend Frances and I are looking into past life regression. We hope to book a session with a professional in Hull in the near future. I hope to God I was someone important in my past life. If I was boring I will just die.

EPILOGUE

I start this concluding part by thanking Sian, a friend of mine who suffers with BPD, for contributing to this final chapter. I asked her for a brief overview of her experience to date, she kindly agreed and her response is below. She was a fantastic Probation Officer and a mentor of mine in the field of supervising offenders subject to Court Orders. Since writing this book both Sian and I have left our jobs in Youth Justice. My decision to do so was not capricious, but decided after much consideration. I needed to put myself first and such a career did not allow this. I wish all my ex-colleagues the best, especially Sian. Below is an email she sent me with regard to her experience of suffering BPD.

Hello Louise, It's me at last!

I was first diagnosed with BPD in September 2000 and was not informed personally about the diagnosis until I read the psychiatric report sent to occupational health in which they were informed and early retirement on health grounds was recommended.

I had no idea what BPD was until I looked it up on the Internet and was horrified!! I have always hated the diagnosis but have to acknowledge that many of my symptoms meet the criteria.

Prior to the diagnosis I was subject to many forms of treatment from 1998 including antidepressants etc. and 38 separate treatments of E.C.T. I was also sectioned under the mental health act and was hospitalised on three occasions. The last in-patient stay was for four months at the end of 2000 and the beginning of 2001.

From 1998 I attended a psychiatric day hospital and continued to do so up until March of this year. I have also had a support worker and social worker but have never attended a support group for other people with a diagnosis of BPD. I have engaged in psychotherapy arranged on the NHS, which is to cease in August 2010.

In terms of coping techniques this has been difficult, hence the intervention of psychiatric services. However, I no longer self harm, am no longer sexually promiscuous and now resist the urge to kill myself.

I am now 61 years old, retired, living in my own property with a long-term friend who is also my carer. I continue to struggle and remain vulnerable. However, my mental health issues never affected my employment for 20 years with the Probation Service and no one ever knew about them.

I am estranged from my family by choice. I have an older sister living in Essex with her family but I have not seen her for 30 years. Both of us have been severely scarred by our formative years. We chose very different routes for our lives and I think I have probably fared much better than her. She did not attend the funerals of our parents and chose the have no contact for her own sanity. I understand this but am very sad that, because of the past, we have not been able to sustain any kind of relationship. I know that my sister would make herself available if needed but she has no idea of my diagnosis.

It is difficult for me to offer advice. I think that because I find accepting the diagnosis so hard I would not be much use to others except to reassure them that they can live a worthwhile life in spite of it.

I feel very sad that I struggled for so long not knowing why I was behaving and reacting to life in the way I was and I feel that I have missed out on many opportunities. I have lived with a load of guilt and now know that I didn't need to keep punishing myself the way I have done all my life.

Take great care of yourself,

Love Sian
x

So where am I now? Am I better? The answer is I am further forward than I was a year ago, but I am not better or cured, I doubt I ever will be. However I am still fighting and I understand and appreciate that I have mental health problems and that they are not going away overnight. I have to take responsibility for my illness and continue to fight. Greg and I still remain together but it is worth noting that prior to me finishing this epilogue we did separate for a short period of time. Whereas I am glad it happened as we are stronger now than ever before, it highlights how difficult it is for partners / carers of those with mental illness. My only advise to anyone emotionally suffering is to only give yourself to a partner who accepts every part of you, including any mental illness you may suffer. I no longer have secrets from Greg, and Maggie was right, true intimacy is fantastic and Greg has really helped me to cope with my illness. Thank you Greg, I love you. In addition, I am much more honest with my parents and to date their support has been paramount. I would like to take this opportunity to thank them for their unconditional love and support. I am lucky to have such good parents.

Flirting With Madness

Currently I still drink too much, binge eat, overspend, feel chronically empty and suffer periods of dissociation but I remain determined to keep going and to date I have made some progress. I am aware that even as I write these words that tomorrow I could sink into a major depression or hit the self-destruct button. However, I choose to fight, it's all I can do.

Take care and keep rocking,

Louise Ellison

xxxx

References

Friedel, R. 'Borderline Personality Disorder Demystified: An Essential Guide for Understanding and Living with BPD.' Marlowe and Company Publishing, New York. 2004.

Kreisman, J and Straus H. 'I Hate You – Don't Leave Me.' Avon Books, New York. 1989.

Kriesman, J and Straus H. 'Sometimes I Act Crazy: Living with Borderline Personality Disorder.' Wiley Publishing, New Jersey, USA. 2004.

Pahlson-Moller, L. 'Little Girl Lost.' Chipmunkapublishing, UK. 2006.

Schwartz, J. 'Brain Lock – Free Yourself from Obsessive Compulsive Behaviour.' Regan Books, New York. 1996.

www.ingramcontent.com/pod-product-compliance
Ingram Content Group UK Ltd.
Pitfield, Milton Keynes, MK11 3LW, UK
UKHW041412180426
11947UKWH00007B/84